All the Thoughts Are Free

Daniel Goodman

ISBN: 1475102461
ISBN-13: 9781475102468

I would like to dedicate these words to my grandsons
Karl-Ashby and Christopher.
Without their love and encouragement,
I never would have been able to tell my story.

• • •

Gerda J. Senner

Table of Contents

Preface

The writing of this book began upon the eighty-fourth birthday of Gerda Senner. Over the past few months, as this date stands, Gerda has had two brain surgeries, suffered a mini stroke, and most recently underwent surgery to remove two counts of skin cancer on her throat and hand. As one will learn from reading the following work, Gerda suffered many hardships in her life, from the most basic and common growing pains, to more intimate and unique experiences that can only be retold, not reenacted. The purpose of this book is not just to relay the tales of Gerda's life, but also to reflect on the compassion and emotion she has shown in each stage of her journey from growing up in Germany, to where she sits today.

As exhibited throughout history, during times of war, people from different places have their own coping mechanisms when confronted with a certain dilemma. One can only be responsible for the applied beliefs and practices that have been learned in their respective environments, only being able to conduct oneself and judge others based on these very experiences. An example of this is the theological struggles that have endured for hundreds of years in different cultures throughout the world. Within these disputes, there is a geographical and spiritual bias relative to blame and accountability. It is unfair to say that one group of people is wrong because of the beliefs they were conditioned to uphold, or to deem someone responsible for actions executed by someone of the same race. Although each of these people may share bonds with each other by means of country, philosophy, or ideology, one can only control and be held accountable for one's own actions. In turn, it is our duty not to look down on fault and misconceptions. Instead, we must marvel at the complete makeup of a person's character and endeavor to understand why they feel the way they do. With hindsight, it is easy to make a humane assessment on these controversial issues, but the subjectivity of a native person or child's immaturity is something that cannot be overlooked, but rather tolerated to some degree.

Such is Gerda's story, a journey with many unforeseen challenges that took her across the globe. She traveled to a slew of places, where she encountered obstacles head on, with the best of her capability and merit. During her upbringing, she was a mere child raised in a time of unique circumstances, with no apparent clues suggesting a tumultuous future, regardless of her precociousness. Hard work and valor were hallmarks of Gerda's life, even in the most troubling of times. After meeting and speaking with Gerda so intimately, for several hours over a number of weeks, many of these deep conversations led to revelations from this unique time period. Three things that surfaced, when she recounted ideals that were withheld in the past, were a sense of regret, compassion, and underlying guilt. These sentiments are not to be conceived in a negative connotation, but rather with the understanding that as a young woman she did not have the means or ability to change the events in Europe during World War II on a grand scale, no matter how much she wished to do so. This displays a shine in her character.

Gerda's story provides not only a different vantage point of Nazi Germany in World War II, but also touches on controversies and troubles not commonly known to the general public. This time period is typically associated with the tragedy and suffering of Jewish people and others at the hand of Adolf Hitler, a maniacal genius who led a purge and fooled a nation into a pilgrimage of death and destruction all in the name of his extreme and erratic philosophies. Less often told is the story of what happened afterwards to the individuals of all of those who were led to believe one thing, only to have their world fall out from beneath them. In the wake of the German surrender, they were faced with a new type of devastation and troubled livelihood. Gerda's life is also a story about the thriving passion of the American dream and how immigrants came to this country not only for the opportunity to build businesses and foundations. America also provided a safe haven and home for people who desperately needed it, and could be said to have offered the ability to live a liberated life away from severe harm more than to the people who were born here.

When reading Gerda's story, make sure to not only acknowledge the value of an individual's life, or to admire the path that hard work and determination can lead to, but also to approach it with a sense of forgiveness and compassion. For the tale of Gerda Senner is one of the survival of a woman who ultimately pursued safety and happiness. Despite living through unimaginably bleak situations that would shatter many, she continued to thrive.

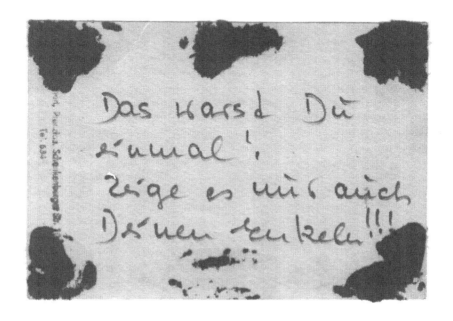

"This was you once! Show your grandchildren one day!!!"

Chapter One

BORN IN WITTENBERGE (1927-1936)

Gerda Suckow

BORN IN WITTENBERGE (1927-1936)

Tucked in between Berlin and Hamburg lies a city in Northeast Germany called Wittenberge. Located on the northern shore of the Elbe River, the city is not to be confused with Wittenberg, a much larger city located nearly 200 kilometers south. In the beginning of the twentieth century, Wittenberge was a city of 20,000 people located in the district of Prignitz. The small town was not on the forefront of political movements, or anything extraordinarily special. Since factories were first built there in the 1800s, Wittenberge provided a number of employment opportunities to man the industry, comprising the town of its blue-collar, traditional working culture. One factory produced rayon ("zellwolle" in German), a synthetic silk and textile made from regenerated cellulose. Since this material exists naturally, the byproduct is also organic, like molasses. Another industry that emerged was through the railway stations known as the Reichsbahn. The maintenance and working mechanics of the railways and factories provided many jobs for the citizens of Wittenberge, including one Otto Suckow.

As a result of his upbringing on his family farm, Otto became a strict and stern man who earned an honest living within the rules. One of five children, Otto had two brothers and two sisters. Most of his siblings grew up to continue farm life in some facet. His two brothers, Wilhelm and Paul, became farmers of their own while one of his sisters, Hertha, also married into the agrarian life. Anna, his youngest sister, outgrew the farm life, and went on to an exciting jet-setting story all her own. For his part, Otto found love in Wittenberge. Otto went on to live in Wittenberge with his wife Minna, a traditional German woman who was very kindhearted. It was there that he would develop his life, taking the values from the farm and the simplicity of the German culture and applying them to his own family.

Otto served in World War I as a soldier for the German military on the front line. His service led him to France where a grenade wounded him during the war. The ejected shrapnel hit his helmet, then blasted to his shoulder and exited at his elbow. Otto's injuries were tended to in an army hospital on the top of a mountain in France, near the battlefield where the event took place. However, he was left there unattended during the crucial time of his trauma, and spent the rest of his life crippled in his left hand. Luckily, he was able to keep the appendage, but it was apparent that there was something wrong. Otto was still able to do many things, whether it was tasks around the house, work, or gardening, a hobby he was especially good at. After his service in the war came to a close, Otto was hired at the Singer Sewing Company, which was built at the turn of the century. The American-based company hired him as a technician and mechanic for machines that helped wind thread. He would work with the spools, making sure that they were well maintained and functional.

Suckow home in Wittenberge

After the war, when Otto settled into his job, he and Minna acted again as the traditional German couple, working honestly, earning a small and modest living, and enjoying their days as they knew they could. On October 20, 1927, they had their first child: a girl they named Gerda. Three years later, they gave birth to their second child, another girl named Hannelore. Life in Wittenberge for the two girls was restrained but pleasant. Otto and Minna were not wealthy and could not afford to buy lavish things, or go on any sort of trip or vacation. But they provided their children with a comfortable home and cared for them well. Although their financial shortcomings were restrictive, the Suckow household was a safe place where the children were compensated in all the proper ways.

In Germany, families held on to the traditional roles of the period. Men supported and protected the family, while it was unheard of for women to work. In addition to raising children, women were expected to keep the household maintained. It was also uncommon for German families to act as affectionate as some are familiar with in the United States or other parts of the world. For example, very few people said, "I love you." Even exchanging a simple hug or kiss was uncommon within families, and Gerda grew up without that physical confirmation of love from her parents. This is not to say that love did not exist in this family, because it did. Otto expressed his affection by working hard and disciplining the girls to become stand-up citizens and ladies. Minna had a loving and caring quality to her that translated through motherhood, solacing the pains of her children in a different light than her husband. Although Minna was not demonstrative, the love she had for her children was always sincere. Together, Otto and Minna made a complete and balanced couple, where Otto would work hard and enforce rules sternly while Minna tended to difficult issues in a calming way.

Gerda and Hannelore

4

The 1920s and 1930s were a time of political unrest and economic struggle in Germany, causing the need for a change of the guard. Still capitalizing in the bitterness from their defeat in World War I, the rising Nazi party implemented a campaign of proclaiming that Germans got "stabbed in the back" by their allies rather than losing the war. Germany was entering a trying time in its efforts to rebound from World War I, and the struggle trickled down to the Suckows. Wittenberge featured newly-instituted industry and a relatively bustling downtown, with shops and stores lining the streets. Gerda and her family frequented these places all their lives including a furniture shop and a convenience store. The furniture store was big and beautiful, with featherbeds and china and all sorts of pretty decorative pieces coating the walls and shelves around the room. The proprietors of each of these stores were Jewish, which Gerda and her family did not see as controversial at the time. They had Jews in their family and the widespread hate and persecution that was promoted did not directly apply to their lives at all times. Before Nazism, the Jewish families were an accepted part of the town without an association with conflict. Although Gerda's family did not know the owners intimately, they had visited the store so much that the Jewish families became a familiar fixture of the town and cordial with most members of the community.

Material things were not a consistent part of the girls' childhood. Minna would dress them frugally by sewing all their clothes. She never went to a store or purchased anything that was not essential to survival. The shoes that Gerda and her sister would wear were rationed by the state. Once a year, the girls would receive shoes and have to adapt to the one size, even as their adolescent feet grew throughout the year. In a successful effort to maximize the life of the rationed items, Minna chose shoes that were too big. She put cotton in the toes at first, so they would fit the young girls. At one point during the year they would fit just right. Later, the shoes became too small, hurting their feet with each step.

The only new purchases that Minna made for her daughters were dresses from the Bleyle Company. This was a special dress, made by a German manufacturer, which was knitted and lasted forever. If the elbows wore out, they would get replaced. If the dress became too short, the garment was sent in to the company where the dress was manufactured and there, tailors would add length, making the dress more of a lasting purchase than an impermanent gift. Material things were never a priority for the Suckow family. As a child, Gerda would have liked to have had new things once in a while. Still, Gerda found happiness in other ways during her childhood.

Every year, Wittenberge hosted a town fair that Gerda looked forward to. It featured carnival-type fare and fun for families of the small town. The carnival had a carousel and a merry-go-round to go along with many other attractions. There were also games for people to play and possibly win prizes. One of the most popular games was the giant wheel. The wheel had many different possible outcomes one could land on. Pony rides, food and other goodies awaited some of the wheel's luckiest spinners. On one occasion, Gerda won a giant smoked eel, a delicacy in this region of the world. It was a big deal to win such a delicious treat and Gerda enjoyed the sensation of winning almost as much as the taste of the smoky eel. Aside from the games and excitement of the attractions, Gerda enjoyed this time with her family and friends.

Gerda also enjoyed going to school, where she excelled in many subjects, except English. For some reason, learning this language was never an interest for her and would always come last in her studies. Gerda read books from the German series "Heidi Goes to America" which featured a young German girl and her adventures across the pond in the United States. This seemed like a dream to Gerda. She imagined herself, like Heidi, traversing across the world to a new land with vast opportunity and exciting adventures. She was captivated by the rolling landscapes and endless possibilities of stories and experiences that awaited her in the States. Despite her lack of achievement in language class, Gerda's burning desire as a child to move to America continued to grow throughout her adolescence. She would always speak to her teachers, classmates and friends about one day making it to America. However, there was one problem that everyone kept alluding to, an obvious obstacle that could not be overlooked: she couldn't speak English! Gerda pleaded that she did not care about the language, and that she was going to go regardless. People laughed at her then, but in Gerda's mind, there was never any doubt that she would inevitably end up in America.

Outside of school, Gerda relished other activities. Bicycles were very popular and from the moment that Gerda's father taught her how to ride, they would go on bike rides all the time together. Whether it was a cruise along the river or through downtown Wittenberge, Gerda sat on her father's handlebars, absorbing the scenery and natural beauty of her small town's proximity to the German countryside. In addition to bicycles, the river situated along the town of Wittenberge provided much entertainment and allure. Fishing through the inlets and walking along the Elbe River were among some of the activities enjoyed by the townspeople.

Gerda on her father Otto's handlebars, 1930.

Gerda had a fondness for the water at a young age, even if she had not known how passionately she would come to love it. At the public pool in Wittenberge they had a set of diving platforms, each being a bit higher than the next. The highest stood at the intimidating height of ten meters. Gerda was always intrigued by the series of high dives. She started with the lowest and slowly worked her way toward the next progression. She had conquered most of the platforms, but the highest one still towered, a bit intimidating for the little girl. She would climb to the very top looking down at the daunting plunge, but could not summon the courage to jump down. Gerda had to be assisted down the platform each time this sequence occurred. On one occasion, her father was fed up with these antics so he climbed up to where Gerda sat perched above the pool and pushed her in, sending her plummeting into the water. As Gerda emerged from the water, she started crying and screaming, not out of pain, but fear and shock. In doing so, she quickly paddled over to the sidewall to catch her breath. The swim coach then quickly approached her. He did not scold her or even seek if she was okay from the fall. Instead, he saw something in Gerda, a natural talent in her panicked stroke, and decided to start training her in swimming.

This was the beginning of Gerda's infatuation with swimming and the water. She began to train with the swim coach at the public pool, perfecting her strokes and becoming a composed and skilled swimmer. Gerda would continue to work on her swimming and practice with other children, using unique tools. One apparatus in particular had a system of tracks and leashes in the pool that enabled the swimmer to train with some resistance, while presenting no risk of drowning or going under the water. Essentially she was in a stationary state of constant swimming. Gerda's swim instructor had a leash or rope tied to Gerda. As she swam, the track moved along with her back and forth to gain strength and speed. Gerda enjoyed swimming, mostly because she was very good at it, and also because it was something that could not be taken away. As long as there was water, there was an opportunity to swim and be happy doing it. In addition to her own personal enjoyment, Gerda had a completely different avenue to meet friends with the same love for the water that she had through joining the swim team. Together, she felt an intimate sense of camaraderie among her teammates who shared the same passion. Swimming not only provided Gerda with an enjoyable hobby, but also would enable greater opportunities later in life through the team and competitions.

Although seemingly commonplace, the setting of a festival or bike ride was a bit different in this part of the world. To Gerda, she was seeing the world as any ten-year-old would: a fun place with many activities and typical happenings of adolescence. However, at this time in history, Germany was undergoing an unprecedented transition that would stretch the limits of humanity and ruthlessness of her country's elected leaders. Gerda's childhood was about to change in ways that she could not comprehend at the time, but would prove to have a lasting effect in history. In 1933, Adolf Hitler had been elected as Chancellor of Germany. Upon taking office, he instilled a state of Nazism that transformed Germany into a genocidal elitist state. Yet, to the general public, life during these elementary stages of political shifting was not telling of such controversy, including not to Gerda.

Chapter Two

LIFE UNDER HITLER (1937-1942)

Before Gerda was born, the seeds of the Nazi political movement were already brewing in Germany. Adolf Hitler began his tirade of propaganda and influence in the decades prior to Gerda's birth. He aimed to make Germany larger, and leave a lasting presence in Europe through Nazism, a philosophy that idolized the prototypical German as an Aryan of blonde hair and blue eyes while extinguishing all other races, most specifically the Jewish people, who he blamed for most of Germany's problems. One way he did this was by conquering other bordering countries and territories in an effort to return them to the "homeland" of Germany. Hitler used the term Lebensraum to contextualize expanding Germany's living space into these territories. This puzzled Gerda because there were plenty of states that Hitler overtook that she did not see having any place in Germany, places that were states all their own. It was clear to Gerda that Austria had some sort of historical affiliation with Germany but she wondered how Czechoslovakia or North Africa could be considered Germany at any point in time. She questioned if these people were truly happy to be "coming home".

The rise of Hitler as a powerful chancellor in Germany is a complex tale that dates back to his younger days as a mere foot soldier for the German infantry. Hitler had a great talent for public speaking and rallying crowds. He often captivated his listeners into not only hearing his ideas, but also agreeing with them no matter how extreme they may have seemed. Eventually, Hitler convinced and persuaded many soldiers to be part of his party's military force known as Sturmabteilung or SA. Wearing all brown uniforms, the so-called "brownshirts" terrorized anyone who opposed or compromised the master plan of Hitler and his followers. Before gaining control of the German army and its government, the brownshirts were the rogue activists that physically enforced Hitler's campaign and rising power. As Hitler's rule escalated, he started not only claiming territories outside Germany as his own, but also collecting and grouping people who were not part of his Nazi agenda into labor camps, where they would work until they were exterminated. These were more commonly known as concentration camps, and are widely understood to not just have had harsh conditions, but also stood as the stations of mass genocide.

Hitler's reign of terror, destruction and death is well known but the Nazi leader was not always perceived as a brilliant monster who exterminated groups of people. Hitler was initially revered and praised by a majority of Germans who elected him into office. He was portrayed as a hero, and had a staff in place that misled the world into believing that he was not conducting himself in an incorrigible manner. From a propaganda minister to the leader of his rogue army, Hitler had all the bases covered so his plan could be executed seamlessly. Although it may be clear in hindsight that Hitler committed unimaginably inhumane crimes, there was not much evidence at the time for the average German to necessarily even second-guess what was happening in their midst, much less revolt or fight back.

On the other hand, many German people benefited from the early stages of Hitler's rise before the war got into full swing - Gerda being one of them. Hitler used his power and reach not with the sole intention to exterminate a certain group of people or conquer other lands, but also to mold Germany into a paradisiacal conception that he theorized in *Mein Kampf*, a manifesto written while jailed that explained his philosophy and master plan. Hitler had a vision of a perfect citizen and society that would symbolize Germany and its people. Taken from mythical influences, the Aryan was a blonde-haired, blue-eyed, fit and intelligent person who would carry out the values of Hitler's utopia. In order to create a country whose only members were exclusive to this make-up, Hitler's vision carried him to not just attempt to wipe out and eliminate those who did not fit the criteria, but cater and facilitate to those who would grow into an Aryan or near perfect German. For this reason, Hitler sought out the best and brightest and created many programs and opportunities for these people, who he prophesized and preached would flourish and procreate so Germany could get closer and closer to that Aryan ideal.

Gerda was always a smart child, working hard to get good grades and naturally better than most of her classmates. But being poor turned out to not only limit the clothes she wore but also what school she could attend - until Hitler. Hitler allowed Gerda a lifestyle and education that was simply out of her family's budget. Through his policy, Hitler granted scholarships for the brightest and best Germans to cater to their skills regardless of economic status, as long as they carried the Nazi agenda. Because of her high test scores and good grades, Gerda was granted this scholarship to a better school, one that was overseen by Hitler. Even though the scholarship was only twenty dollars, the money was significant for the family at the time, no matter how small that amount seems today. Gerda's sister Hannelore did not get such a scholarship and did not attend the same school as her older sister. Gerda felt privileged to be able to attend such a school. The faculties at these schools were required by Hitler to have a PhD in order to teach, even for physical education. Each child would receive a large cylindrical cone filled with goodies and treats to start the school year.

Gerda at her first day of school

11

One of Hitler's tools in further achieving the goal to promote Nazism and the Aryan race was creating the Hitler Youth. Unlike school, the Hitler Youth was a supplemental organization designed to groom and educate German children in regards to strictly Nazism, developing them into outstanding new citizens for the vision of an ideal Germany that Hitler foresaw. Therein lies Gerda: finding her stride on the swim team while gallivanting with friends on bicycles through annual fairs and forging gleeful childhood memories. In addition to her new school, upon Gerda's tenth birthday, she and all other German boys and girls were enlisted in the Hitler Youth. At the time, it was completely normal and expected of children to enter this group; there was no choice in the matter, nor a reason to contest it.

Besides educating the youth at the highest level, the program also groomed the children into upstanding German citizens of the new Reich. The Hitler Youth was not coed, splitting the boys and girls into Gymnasium and Lyzeum respectively. The boys were subjected to more physical training and the girls were taught more sentimental lessons associated with femininity and compassion. The girl's division, where Gerda was enlisted, was called the BDM (Bund Deutscher Madel), meaning the league of German girls. Gerda loved the uniforms for the Hitler Youth, which was an entirely different look than she was accustomed to. They wore brand new white shirts with blue skirts and a tied cord-like rope hanging from the neck. The color of the leather cord depicted their role or status among the BDM. Gerda was a model Aryan girl at the time, performing well in school and other extracurricular activities. She excelled in her studies and on the swim team and exhibited the exact attributes that were sought for the BDM. For once, her family's economic shortcomings were irrelevant. In time, Gerda was bestowed a green cord indicating she was a leader among the group. But even with the great opportunity that was provided for Gerda, her father Otto was not completely receptive. He always had a problem with the Nazi party and in turn the Hitler Youth.

*One of Gerda's friends from the Hitler Youth
wearing uniform and cord.*

Otto did not want his daughters to be in the Hitler Youth because he did not believe in Nazism, and sneered at the praise of Hitler. There were many people who had similar sentiments as Otto. Due to the widespread power the Nazis possessed and the severity of their enforcement, resisting the movement would be a foolish move. Hitler's rise to power was slow and steady, and all resistors were usually countered violently. No matter how much Otto opposed the SA and its movement, he could not do anything meaningful due to the power and stronghold it had over the country. Otto shared ideologies with the older people of Germany, not buying into the radical claims of this young unaccomplished political figure. Otto did not embrace the rapid climb of Hitler, but rather scoffed at his platform and the devout allegiance from the more youthful activists in Germany. He had personal reasons as well for opposing Hitler.

Otto was once arrested by the SA for visiting his Jewish relative, and knew the severity of getting himself and his family involved in a political conflict. His sister Anna married a full-blooded Jew, a wonderful man of fine character who was forced to leave Germany as Hitler ordered the exile of the Jewish people. Otto went to see the couple in their new home in Switzerland and was arrested upon his return for visiting a Jew. Though Otto's brother-in-law was not his immediate family, the SA did not regard any condition suitable when considering the Jewish people and those associated to them. Otto, like many, had to suppress his feelings as long as the SA was in power.

Along with two other girls on scholarship, Gerda entered the Hitler Youth with the same sense of excitement that one would have on the first day of school. She knew the other children, as everyone was going to be in Hitler Youth and thought nothing of partaking in the program. She continued to work hard in school as she always had, while still enjoying her life as any young girl would. Everyone she knew was in Hitler Youth, but not everyone got this prestigious scholarship at such a tender age. Even though, at least in Hitler's eyes, Gerda was among the elite Germans, others continued to bully her for being poor. Kids would make fun of her father, and at times chase her down the street calling her names. They were constantly teasing her for the cheap clothes she wore or her father's job, saying anything to get under her skin. Gerda learned that as much as Hitler had brought her close to her friends, kids ultimately can be cruel. Even if Hitler had seen them as equal, the children too young to comprehend this would continue to ridicule and torment her.

Gerda on a school trip to Borkum, an island in the North Sea, 1937

One traumatic day left a glaring impression on Gerda regarding her economic status when she attended a friend's birthday party. Gerda was so excited to be invited to the party that her mother got the best present that she could manage to afford. Gerda put on her finest dress and headed to the party with the gift, eager to meet new friends, eat sweets and enjoy the festivities with her peers. Upon arriving to the party, the girl's mother took the gift from Gerda and quickly pulled her aside. The mother told Gerda that she could not enter the party because she had lice. Gerda pleaded with the woman to let her stay, saying she had never had a louse in her life. She just wanted to go play with the other children. The mother refused and forced her to leave, keeping the gift. Gerda ran home crying to her mother and realized that the reason for this treatment was again because of being poor. Her family's poverty was an obstacle for Gerda that she always dealt with on her own. But as the bullying went even further than the children, with parents enabling the ridicule, it in turn created more difficulties for Gerda to overcome.

No matter where the location or period of time, it seems that status and bullying are always a part of people's lives, Gerda included. Bullying was not the foundation of Gerda's childhood, though. The Hitler Youth had a greater agenda, one that held precedent over the common ridicule that children endured. The children of the Hitler Youth were influenced greatly in their training to praise Hitler. They were required, like other Germans, to heil Hitler as a salutation. This meant to stop, raise your right arm, and declare "Heil Hitler!" Gerda did not think much of this at the time and would salute people in this manner without even considering exactly what was being suggested. It was not just an acknowledgment of Hitler, but validation for the SA and Third Reich's agenda.

A good student before Hitler Youth, Gerda thrived under the exciting new organization she and her peers were a part of. Oddly, Gerda recalls that the Hitler Youth did not educate children on the inner workings of Hitler's master plan to exterminate Jews, or even persecute them. Instead, the only ideologically-influenced teachings the children received challenged the philosophy of Communism as represented by the Russians. It was repeatedly drilled into the children that these Eastern ideals were wrong. Aside from the suggestive propaganda, Gerda recalled much to be excited about regarding the Hitler Youth program, including the camaraderie, activities, and amenities offered.

LIFE UNDER HITLER (1937-1942)

The Hitler Youth would meet after school once a week in big groups of like kids to learn a myriad of songs and marches with nationalistic proclamations. Gerda learned nearly 200 songs to sing-a-long and march to, mostly promoting Nazism and Germany. As a group of children, this was the greatest atmosphere in the world to be a part of: singing, marching, laughing and dancing with other children and friends. The BDM and the rest of the Hitler Youth were having the time of their lives, treated with the finest amenities and all the while made to feel respected and elite. Cleverly, everything was made to seem like a fun game. The children were taken to fairs and rallies to showcase these newly-learned songs as if performing a concert, without realizing the suggestive message of the tunes. Gerda felt special, showcasing her skills and singing in front of such audiences, who cheered loudly and screamed in excitement. The activities committed by the Hitler Youth were anything but scandalous to the children.

The BDM would also do compassionate things like tend to and entertain wounded soldiers. The soldiers were not mangled or too badly hurt by the time they got to Wittenberge, so the horror of war was not apparent quite yet for Gerda. She felt privileged and self satisfying to help in what little ways she could, not curious as to *why* these soldiers were injured, or even fighting. Gerda and her fellow BDM girls went to hospitals to cheer up the soldiers wounded from the front line of the ongoing war. They would sing songs, read them stories, or do anything that children could to cheer up somebody who is hurt. One thing that stood out to Gerda was the age of the soldiers. As the years of the war rolled by, the soldiers seemed to be recycling to Gerda, with different, successively younger men replacing them after each bout. As the battles waged on, it looked almost as if children had replaced the men.

Along with her BDM program, Gerda also enjoyed her time with her normal studies. Gerda excelled at school, which led to her scholarship, but was not the only activity in which she was gifted. From that first day when she was pushed into the pool off the high dive, Gerda continued to gain strength as a swimmer and earned a spot on many teams within the city, school and within the Hitler Youth. Her favorite stroke was the breaststroke, which at the time included the form of the butterfly stroke as well. One would do the butterfly stroke until he was too tired and then would continue with the traditional motions of the breaststroke where today they are two separate distinct strokes.

Through the Hitler Youth, Gerda traveled all over Europe to compete. From Austria to Czechoslovakia to Poland, which were all slowly becoming part of the German homeland under Hitler, Gerda experienced a lifestyle she could not afford. One of her most memorable trips was when she went to Prague, the Golden City, and marveled at the landscape. Gerda was in awe of its sloping hills and the Vltava, the river in Prague that merged with the Elbe from her hometown, slowly snaking under the many bridges. Gerda did not realize that a city could be so breathtaking. Ironically, Prague's beauty was so well preserved because Hitler deemed the city untouchable. His plan was to keep the Jewish quarter of the city as a walking museum for the extinguished Jewish race. As a result, the intricate synagogues and architectural wonders of the city were left untouched unlike the remainder of the country.

At these swimming competitions, Gerda was surrounded by many children who, like herself, were applying their talents in the pool amid a time of war. She went on to win many medals for her accomplishments as a swimmer while all the time gaining exposure to the world. Despite Hitler's iron fist, Gerda was content and saw opportunity in her version of Europe. As long as she said Heil Hitler, there were not many restrictions on her life, and success was not only possible, but in her grasp. She competed with groups of friends at the highest level, at one point even set to train for the Olympics. The chaotic intensity of World War II curtailed her training, but Gerda still met many different people and gained a plethora of memories and positive experiences with her swim program. All her successes and good times, however, were shadowed by the imminent conflict in Europe. As Gerda entered adolescence, tensions were escalating between Western allies and the Third Reich, amounting in a chaotic warzone that greatly limited any chance of a normal livelihood.

In a way, Gerda held the highest status of those she competed against, being a part of the Nazi plan. She did not realize it at the time, but most of the children she competed against were likely not as happy as she was. They did not get to sing songs and march with friends, but were rather under the thumb of the very Reich she was trained to support. It is a bit frightening to extrapolate what happened to all these random children that Gerda encountered throughout her travels. Some of them likely went on to be imprisoned in labor camps, and were detached from their families. Perhaps one of the children had a unique story of escape and survival. In contrast, Gerda's time on the swim team, the years she spent in an esteemed school, and her days during the Hitler Youth singing songs and marching were among some of the happiest times of her life. Objectively, they were all a little girl could want, in stark contrast to her opponents.

But at home there was an indication that all was not as rosy as these songs depicted. Her father still did not approve of Hitler. Otto saw him as a crazy man, and would grow angry when speaking about his erratic ways and abrasive rise to chancellor. Naturally, Otto's views conflicted with Gerda's teachings at school. One of the duties of Hitler's army and in turn the Youth was to keep an ear out to those who opposed the Third Reich and report those who were considered a threat with the execution of his master plan. On one occasion, when Gerda's father was speaking badly of Hitler, she told him: "If you say another word about Hitler, I am going to report you!" Her father had a look of dumbfounded shock, as if he just saw something unimaginable. Gerda stood angrily, speaking as candidly and seriously as a twelve-year-old girl could, almost in a scorning tone. It was not for hatred, but because she was indoctrinated to react this very way.

To Gerda, it seemed like the right thing to do at the time. The consequence of reporting someone for speaking ill of Hitler was not laid out, nor was the severity of the punishment. Looking back, Gerda realized that she was so engrossed in the Hitler Youth philosophy, which she was preconditioned to uphold, that she unknowingly threatened her own family. The action speaks volumes not only to the power of Hitler Youth, but also how brainwashed and ignorant Gerda was at the time. Gerda was programmed to prioritize her life with the Hitler Youth agenda at the top, even at the expense of her own family. Never again did Otto speak that way in front of his little girl, out of fear of what could happen. It is also amazing to think what he must have been feeling at that moment, when your own family member does not understand the *real* terrors occurring in Germany, or the person who posed the greatest threat.

In 1938, when Gerda was first adjusting to her role in the Hitler Youth as an 11-year-old girl, she experienced something that was eerily beautiful. On a warm November night, Gerda's father asked her to walk downtown with him. Gerda agreed. She was unsure why he chose not to ride bicycles, but was nevertheless more than happy to take a stroll with her father. As they approached the downtown streets, Gerda was confused and tickled by the fluttering of snowflakes across the night sky. Gerda questioned why it was snowing at a time when it was not very cold, but at first she did not suspect anything peculiar. She was engulfed in the majesty of the scene at hand. Skipping and trotting through the snow, Gerda stepped over broken pieces of porcelain and crystal, glittering in the streets. The combination of the snow and china created a fantasyland that was nothing less than magical to the young girl.

The snow was puzzling, but that made it all the more mystical. The china on the floor usually meant someone was getting married. In a German tradition called Polterabend, friends and family of the couple-to-be throw and break china, crystal, and porcelain for good luck. The Germans believed that the broken pieces or shards brought good luck. Gerda knew that the nicer china brought the best luck, not the cheap stuff. But Gerda also noticed some peculiar things that might have not been aligned with a world of fantasy and beauty that she was experiencing. She saw the brownshirts running around from place to place, but no other people. She wondered where everyone else was. There were *only* brownshirts running around. There was no sense of sincerity or emotion that she could see from the people rustling. Gerda did not see anyone crying or even reacting to all the things being broken. Something was different. This beautiful walk with her father was memorable for Gerda. But only later did she learn the true reason for its significance.

Gerda's stroll was in fact through Kristallnacht, a nationwide pogrom. Hitler ordered his army to destroy all the businesses and possessions of Jews throughout Germany. Translated into English as "the night of broken glass", this was no fantastic experience. The snow that Gerda had every reason to question was actually countless feathers from the beds, pillows, and furniture, belonging to the Jewish people of her town, that were torn and tattered and thrown out the windows, creating a flurry of light-colored feathers dancing through the sky. The broken dishes on the ground were the contents of the Jewish people's homes and businesses. After that night, the Jewish people of Wittenberge were left with nothing but fear, tears and uncertainty about the future. Where before he ruled with less overt tactics, Hitler took a stand on that night, showing the German Jews that they were not in control of their lives anymore. He tried to force them to abide by Nazi principles.

The Jewish people never stood out to Gerda, but now she grew to notice the paraphernalia they wore, and their roles as decided by Hitler in the new world that he created for them. Gerda never gave any

19

thought to the gold stars worn on some people's clothing that noted they were Jewish. She saw no harm in wearing such a thing, heeding no suggestive implications in the flare. In fact, if Gerda were given a gold star saying she was German, she would have worn it. But the Jews were forced to wear the stars, and they came with insinuations of ostracism, and other negative connotations. After Kristallnacht, the storefront of the convenience store where her family would often visit was completely destroyed, with nothing left but shattered glass and debris. This was the first glimpse outside of her life that alluded to the nefarious forces beyond. Now, there was something that had the town and her family on edge, something that was not directly taught in her Hitler Youth classes. If anything, this confused the little girl. All the implications and symbolism of these ruthless and hateful activities were too strenuous and complex for someone so young to understand. Regardless, this was a night that she would never forget.

Chapter Three

YEARS OF WAR (1942-1945)

Over the next few years, the conflict between Germany and Eastern Europe began to intensify, resulting in the declaration of World War II. Countries from the West and East chose sides and began formulating their own military agendas to battle Hitler. This had a duel effect in Gerda's life, not only creating an environment of hostility and destruction, but also changing the pace and makeup of everyday life and activities within Germany. No matter how ignorant people were to the details of this ongoing war, the physical and military threat was always the most jarring, creating a chaotic state where school schedules, working routines, and other everyday affairs were derailed. People were aware of what was happening, but at the same time tried to live their own lives and pursue their tasks in school or work. Regardless of any plan one has in life, if there is bombing and destruction around, preserving one's life will always take priority. Hitler began to collude with Soviets and Japanese allies as the West was forming their own alliances. The German people continued their lives under the guise that Germany was winning and Nazism was in the beginning stages of its prosperous thousand-year reign.

Gerda understood no different. After six years of schooling, German students had an opportunity to continue their studies in a trade school or apprenticeship, to segue into their desired profession. During her studies, Gerda gained an interest in chemistry. She loved to conduct experiments, fascinated with the practicum and analysis, attempting to figure out how compounds and tangible things were formed, by mixing and combining different materials. Gerda's close friend shared the same passion as her, and together they enjoyed working through chemistry. Gerda elected to take an internship at the rayon factory in town. Once again, Hitler's policies had enabled Gerda to realize her dream, providing her with an opportunity to learn and grow in the field she aspired to be a part of.

Gerda and her colleague, a female chemist who mentored her during her apprenticeship, rode their bicycles to their job at the factory, each day with sandwiches packed for lunch. At the factory, they conducted experiments with the synthetic cloth and its byproducts, as well as other types of projects. Near the factory was another large building that resembled a college dormitory. From behind the gated fence, Gerda and her friend peered through to see the workers mixing and cleaning out chemicals from the building. They heard the workers speaking different languages, and realized they were not all German. The men looked boyish and weak, making it difficult to guess what age they actually were.

Gerda and her friend decided they wanted to do something nice for the workers, seeing these men working all day in what was apparently a tough job. The girls began to pack some extra sandwiches for the laborers, made with the molasses byproduct from the rayon factory. They would ride their bicycles over to the men, and hand them the food through the gates. The men quickly gobbled up the treats as if it was the first time they tasted a sandwich. The girls continued packing and bringing lunches to the men for much of their time working at the rayon factory. All the while, Gerda and her friend did not suspect why the workers were indeed so famished.

While working as a chemist, she and many of the German townspeople were unaware of the extreme measures of ongoing genocide being carried out by Hitler. At this point, Hitler's mission to ethnically cleanse Germany of the Jewish people had escalated to a frightening level. Nearly every Jew in Germany and its neighboring countries would be extinguished by gas chambers, or other forms of execution under Hitler's orders. Hitler had created a number of concentration camps where foreigners and Jews were imprisoned and forced into labor for the Third Reich and from there, would be executed in a number of ways.

Just as Gerda was settling into her position at trade school, these camps were being established across Germany, Poland, and the Czech Republic or some other areas of the new Germany - the homeland Hitler continued to expand. The conditions in these camps varied, as there were more than 1500 locations, all poor to some degree. There was often no insulation, which was especially brutal in the frigid winter months in Germany. The camps lacked amenities like toilets and fresh clothes, and food was scarce, hovering just above complete starvation. The prisoners endured these hardships, usually after being separated from their families, until they were no longer viewed as useful, and then killed. By the end of the war, the camps were responsible for nearly half the deaths of the 6,000,000 Jews and 5,000,000 people of other races who were not in line with the Aryan ideal.

In Wittenberge, a small concentration camp existed that was associated with the larger Neuengamme concentration camp located in Hamburg. Although it was not one of the notorious camps that live on in history, the camp in Gerda's hometown conducted the same types of activities and horrors that were happening across the country to the Jewish people and other prisoners. They were forced into labor, often fixing German machinery, building artillery and weapons, or, as Gerda and her friend observed, cleaning up a factory. These prisoners were of the very same that Gerda unassumingly shared her lunches with. Gerda and her friend packed lunch for the workers not knowing that for some it could have been their last meal. She remembers it as an ingenuous task, but to these laborers, it surely may have meant more.

When first entering the Hitler Youth in 1937, Gerda was a very young girl with an impressionable mind. She loved Hitler for making her dreams come true and facilitating the happier moments of her childhood. One time after she saw Hitler in Berlin, she described him like a magnet, drawing everyone in to him, enamored and eager. But as she was maturing into a young woman and Hitler's plan was coming to fruition, the country suffered from it, along with her family. As a result, her opinion gradually moved toward that of her father's. Along with the rapidly morphing state of her hometown, things were starting to take a turn for the worst all over Germany, due to the progressive involvement of British and American armies in the war.

As the years went by and Gerda was moving toward graduating from her apprenticeship and beginning her career as a chemist, the war continued to grow more tenuous. Germany had become an embedded warzone with bombings, conflict and destruction at nearly every turn. The SA and the German army continued its imperialistic mission of persistent expansion. Germany was approaching the size of Texas.

In turn, Hitler's army was wearing thinner as more conflict brought more casualties. Hitler's soldiers were getting younger and younger. Additionally, other countries around the world were beginning to realize what was happening in Germany and began to intervene- first politically, then with force.

The escalation of violence was due partly to Hitler's actions against the Soviet Union and the rest of Eastern Europe. In 1939, Adolf Hitler and Soviet Premier Joseph Stalin signed a non-aggression pact, which stated that neither side would fight against each other while their imperialistic agendas were carried out. Under this agreement, the two also decided to secretly split the occupation of Poland between them, with Germany taking the West and the Soviet Union taking the East. Upon Germany's invasion of Poland, the United Kingdom and France entered the war as allies against the third Reich and Hitler's reign. For Gerda, this signified the beginning of living on a war front yet she remained ignorant to the true happenings and details of the conflict.

In the beginning stages of the war, Germany instituted a system of rations for its citizens. They were given a system similar to food stamps in order to attain food, cigarettes and other everyday necessities. The local convenience stores held a certain amount of goods to distribute to each citizen every week. Since Wittenberge was quite small, there was not much controversy over the allotted items, as it was nearly impossible to get more than one was allocated. Gerda did not smoke cigarettes before the rations but eventually took up the habit due to the inherent value the items held in its scarcity. "Why should someone else get them if this was the only thing you could possess?" Gerda thought. The habit did not last long.

In addition to rationing, the country's resources were dwindling due to the fact that Germany simply did not have the finances or means to keep up with the rapid growth of Hitler's war machine. This was unknown to Germans because Goebbels was successfully doing his job to absolve any suspicion or doubt among its people. Things would continue to get progressively worse as the war reached its close, but during this time, Gerda and the German people were led to believe there was no cause for concern.

The country's psyche during the war went beyond that of patriotism and allegiance to the Reich. Due to the influential strategies of propaganda, the German people, at first, wanted to fight, and in doing so, overlooked the poor conditions that rationing would infer. While waiting in line for her bread and cigarettes, Gerda recalls men chanting "Bombs, not butter!" Clearly, the government was not rationing bombs, but the people's desire for more ammunition rather than sustaining food was apparent. This alluded to the hazy mindset of the German people from the fog of war, where they had been coaxed into accepting and praising the unfit economic conditions of the state. Gerda, on the other hand, would take her bread and butter and eat it all as soon as she got her hands on it. At these times, she did not know how sparingly meals would come or if she would live to see her next meal at all. In turn, she took advantage of any handout or ration.

Some German people fully supported the Nazis in their fight to propel Germany toward a surge of prosperity. Gerda recalled the range of different men she encountered in this stage of her life. There was the desperate fanatics, who lived for destruction and national pride, and the young soldiers who were killed or suffering on the front line. The experiences of Nazism for the German people were respectively different from case to case. These men met different fates, both in the name of Nazism, a faltering movement. Gerda did not have the same invigorated spirit as these other men possessed, instead longing for the trauma to end.

As pressure from the West was ever growing, Hitler's own devious and selfish military tactics led to even more pressure from what were once his own allies. In opposition to the details of the non-aggression pact previously signed with the Soviet Union, Hitler planned to invade Russia, the very country that he promised he would not. Stalin was warned by the United States, the United Kingdom, as well as from his own Soviet spies about Hitler's plans of invasion. Even with two years of knowledge and preparation for the attack, the Soviet Union simply did not have the manpower or modern artillery to compete with Germany's invading forces. After Germany invaded Russia, there was little stopping the force as they marched all the way to Moscow, frightening the Soviet people, brutally killing scores along the way. After much resistance, Stalin decided that it was time to take action against the maniacal Hitler, who clearly exhibited no trustworthy integrity and must be stopped before his own state was completely conquered.

In the coming years after the first order of Germany's invasion of Russia in 1940, the Soviet forces started to dissipate as Hitler and his army began to have a stronger presence. In 1943, the leaders of the Soviet Union, the United Kingdom and the United States met in Tehran to discuss how to approach what had then become World War II. During this meeting of the big three that included Joseph Stalin, Winston Churchill, and Franklin Delano Roosevelt, the allies decided to leave their contradicting communistic and democratic philosophies aside, and vowed to fight against Germany and the Third Reich until Hitler's empire and Nazism were defeated. Although this was a move in the right direction to world peace, for Gerda and Wittenberge this simply meant more aggression and looming violence.

Even as the perils of war became apparent, with bombs continually dropping and the German people dying on the front line, Gerda and others were told of the one weapon that would change the course of the war. It was a piece of artillery that would end all their struggles, a game-changer more powerful than anyone had ever seen or imagined. These "wonder weapons," or wunderwaffe in German, referred to extreme tools of destruction. Goebbels spread this idea to the German people, and in turn they faithfully believed that with one stroke, Germany would prevail by effect of this devastating weapon. A German nuclear team developed such a weapon, the atomic bomb. However, it was not for Germany. Americans had German nuclear technicians create the bomb for them, in fact, and this secret weapon that Goebbels and Hitler touted was never used by or for the Nazis. This was yet another example of the misleading propaganda that the German people were subjected to, further invigorating their spirit in the war and faith behind the Nazi regime.

In contrast was the evidence flying overhead, claiming major cities of Germany: bombs of all sorts. Gerda's town had become a war zone. Day after day, more and more bombs were being deployed. There was no end in sight, or way to figure out exactly what was happening, due to the restrictions of the media by Goebbels. From the moment the West declared war, Gerda entered the most traumatic period of her life. She encountered the truth and realness of a war zone.

Gerda and the rest of her family were in a state of perpetual preoccupation as the bombs began to fall in the early 1940's on Wittenberge. After the British and American militaries officially entered the war, they made their presence known with force from above. For Gerda, it is truly painful to relive the horrors of war, looking back at life during this time. She remembered every day as a new challenge to avoid being killed, whether it was by means of running, hiding, or working to maintain some glimmer of hope. Without any education on the subject, Gerda was able to differentiate between the many types of bombs that were used against Germany. There were the normal bombs that would simply drop and explode, destroying anything in their range. The scarier bomb, the weapon that still haunts Gerda to this day, was the phosphorous bomb. These incendiary weapons almost had a mind and personality of their own. They came down like fire, engulfing anything in their sprawling reach. The incendiary bombs would release flaming streams, eating anything they touched from walls to brick to people.

Unfortunately for Gerda, her family, and the town of Wittenberge, they were more victims of geography than the main target of the opposing side's ammunition. Wittenberge is conveniently located in between Berlin and Hamburg. Since these major cities were primary targets for attack, Wittenberge was en route after the planes' trips to hit their targets. On the way out of German territory, the American and British planes would empty the remaining contents that were not dropped on these cities. Wittenberge saw a disproportionate amount of bombs due to this fact.

When the American forces began to bomb Germany in the early 1940s, Gerda and her family had only one thought: to run. Even though the Western forces could have been perceived as the good guys in this conflict, attempting to defeat the Nazis, to the Suckows, they were the ones causing destruction. When someone is shooting and bombs are going off, the only reaction, whether natural or forced, is to run away. Gerda's father reacted quickly, hastily packing up what little things they had and beginning to trek east toward Gerda's grandmother's home, which was presumably safe from the attacks coming from the West. Tying all of their featherbeds to their bicycles, this act combined the family's only worthy possessions and means of transportation. The featherbeds would provide warmth and some sort of shelter for their evacuation, wherever they had to rest. Together as a family, they would ride along the railroads past the special artillery mounted on trains or other platforms, designed to shoot down the planes dropping all the weapons and bombs, called flak. Occasionally stopping at air raid shelters where they could hopefully avoid the bombs for a moment and rest, the Suckows were always fleeing and moving to what they assumed was safe territory. This objective is much more difficult than theorized given the lack of resources, finances, and seemingly vast sprawl of opposing military.

There were a few logical strategies to escape the attacks that continually occurred everyday for years until 1945. For Gerda's family, there was a divide in how to approach the state of war. Gerda's father, Otto, was against Hitler and his movement from the first time he was introduced to the Nazi's erratic politics. He despised the war and already suffered in his arrests and inability to live his life as he wanted. In a way, the war did not seem to scare her father, Gerda observed. It was almost as if he anticipated it, calming in its action. Minna and Hannelore, on the other hand, were terrified and always choosing to hide. Hannelore was always a bit submissive with her actions and emotions, marching to a different beat than her sister. During these trying times, Hannelore sought solace in her mother. They curled under the shelters clenching each other in what could have been their last moments together. Gerda and her father decided that they were not going to go below the trenches or barricades to avoid the bombs like the rest of their family. They feared that if a bomb were to hit, suffocation would be the cause of death, which is much more horrific and painful than dying instantly. Instead, Gerda stood with her father looking up at the sky, ready to take the blow from the bomb head on. They would rather die knowingly than suffer a fate worse than the war had already created.

Waiting became a morbid game for Gerda and her father. She would stare up at the commotion in the sky, counting the American planes soaring overhead. When the first place in line lit up, she knew the bombs were about to come. Gerda would peer through the sky lighting up amid the numbers of barrage balloons, strategically put in place to prevent low flying aircraft. For Gerda, most things in her life that seemed pretty or nice would be twisted or tainted into a negative connotation during the war. Like the fluttering snow during Kristallnacht, these balloons reminded her of the fair where she once won the smoked eel. This image was short-lived, as she realized that there was no aesthetic function for these balloons other than to counter the countless amounts of bombs and planes that soared overhead. It cannot be stressed strongly enough that this was not a rare or short-lived experience. This was something that happened every single day.

After a few months, it became muddled and irrelevant whether Russians or Americans were causing the destruction. For Gerda and her family, the only concern was to stay safe and unharmed, whether that meant running eastward from the Western forces or retreating back toward their home in Wittenberge while fleeing from the Red Army of the Soviet Union. Gerda and her family returned from their escape toward the east as the Soviet army was in the middle of its own battles with the German forces. It seemed that every direction had some sort of resistance toward the Third Reich. The Suckows were always caught in the middle with nowhere to turn. For years, Gerda began to lose faith in many things as she was experiencing the terror of war. In contrast to the beauty she perceived during Kristallnacht, being a teenager during a time of unmistakable violence made her more aware of the true evils existing in the world. Gerda grew to naturally loathe war, fearful in the roots of her emotion toward any enemy that directly threatened her life. The realness of destruction and death was constantly surrounding her. Experiencing these traumas daily as a young girl, a vapid quality began to replace Gerda's hopefulness, with no improvements ever seeming to occur in the state of their lives or safety.

Not all of Gerda's war experience was shared with her family. Gerda's talents as a swimmer reached the highest levels throughout her upbringing, amounting to a chance to train for a spot on the national team in the forthcoming Olympic games. While training for the Olympics in Berlin on one occasion, Gerda experienced one of the most terrifying events in her life. In the middle of swim practice, sirens began to bellow, indicating the beginning of an air raid attack. Gerda and the rest of her team quickly rushed to the air raid shelter where the walls were bordered with ceramic benches. Away from her father, Gerda could not go out to face the bombs, but had to follow the standard procedure and go with the group during the attack. As her swim team packed into the room, the door firmly locked shut behind them. For the next few hours, nothing but rumbling entered the room. The shelter shook furiously from the cacophonic raucous as all the children, from the very young to late teenagers, clenched each other's hands, crying and praying. Although the shelter was structurally sound, holding up for the period of attack, the feeling inside that room was terrifying, with nowhere to hide or run. Gerda waited for something devastating to happen, or for the bombings to stop.

Gerda and friends at swim practice.

The raid eventually subdued, and the children slowly teetered outside of the shelter onto the streets. They slowly approached the sightlines of Berlin with their coaches leading the way. The image was a scene that would be etched in Gerda's mind for the rest of her life. Billows of smoke slowly accumulated, looking as if they were growing like a science experiment gone awry. Rubble and broken bricks were scattered among the streets. Bodies were everywhere and the smell of burning consumed the air. Planes glided low near the streets, deploying bombs that exploded buildings and homes upon impact right in front of the group of children. Gerda saw sections of Berlin destroyed in an instant. The phosphorous bombs followed to reduce whatever was left to ash. The juxtaposition of her swim team's enjoyment and the devastating attack created a perplexing emotion for Gerda, one that weighed heavily on her. She had to reach for strength to persevere through these trying times.

Wittenberge and the rest of Germany soon become chaotic as Gerda's own experiences muddled into a swirl of running and survival. It was impossible to approach school, work, and any other daily activities in a normal way. Even the most optimistic people could not convince or fool themselves into thinking that things were alright. Food was rationed, buildings were being destroyed, people were dying, and above it all, the media portrayed Germany as winning and everything as just fine. Schools and jobs were no longer a priority or secure. Instead, people's lives were at stake. Gerda's apprenticeship, which she enjoyed so much, came to a halt as the fiery attack on the very building she worked in left everything in complete disarray. Gerda was growing more than a distaste for war – she developed a hopelessness and desperation for it to end. With Hitler came opportunity and promises of prosperity for Gerda and the German people. Now, her dreams and livelihood had blended into a hectic state of war that had become her daily life. Hitler's empty promises and the suffering made Gerda yearn for it all to stop.

Prayer and religion started to play a smaller role in the Gerda's life as the war's effects intensified. Gerda could not understand how God could enable or allow all this terror to occur. She grew up in a Lutheran home and although her family was not devout, she understood that there must be some good in God, who should intervene in a situation like this. Gerda could not help but feel a lack of faith begin to fester, seeing terrors and traumas everyday that showed no signs of slowing down or stopping.

One experience in particular was the turning point in her lifelong journey of faith. She went to the factory where she was working, not prepared for the indelible images she would witness. Gerda went to help clean the destruction levied by the dreaded incendiary bombs. Approaching the factory, an obtrusive, pungent odor wafted in her direction. As she walked in the door and saw the main floor of the factory, where she was used to conducting experiments and learning the ins and outs of chemistry, there were dead, burnt, and corroding bodies scattered across the floor, releasing an intense stench.

Gerda helped carry the bodies out of the factory. One by one, she would heave the stinking corpses over her shoulder and carry them outside, piling the charred bodies into one symbolic mass of the veracity of the war. Gerda carried sixteen bodies outside of the factory. In this moment, she realized the horrific power of the phosphorous bombs, and the war's unforgiving destruction. Looking at the pile of the burnt dead, Gerda made a decree to God. It was at this moment when she thought that any deity that would facilitate such a horror could not be something righteous or worth following. This created a void in her life, losing hope in her own future against the tolls of war. But this event was not the conclusion to Gerda's war experience. The bombings and destruction relentlessly continued, simply affirming her new lack of faith.

Gerda's psyche was also starting to take a toll. When she first entered the Hitler Youth a few years earlier, she was having the time of her life: traveling with the swim team, singing and marching with friends, being honored as a leader of her group. Now she found herself as a sixteen-year-old girl who is looking at death in the face every day. At this point, Gerda no longer had the same feeling of togetherness and prosperity she once embraced. Her dreams of being a chemist were clearly out of reach. The quaint town that she grew up in was nearly demolished and ruined. Family, friends, and compatriots were dying in all different ways in all types of places. Gerda just wanted it all to stop.

Another lasting image of the war came upon her family's return to Wittenberge from East Germany. Gerda's father, Otto, was adamant about bringing the featherbeds back from their initial escape to Gerda's grandmother's house in the East. Whether it was money or function, or to keep his family's mind off the intense trauma that surrounded them, these items seemed very important to him, Gerda thought. He would not stop obsessing about those featherbeds. After first leaving the West because of the American's attack, Gerda's family was now fleeing from the Soviet soldiers coming from the East. The German military was also leaving the East, as the Soviets were gaining speed in their assault.

Gerda noticed that many of the men who once proudly served Germany were now responding in the most cowardly of ways as broken men, retreating and halting their efforts. She saw that the men had rags tied around their feet, as their shoes had been withered and destroyed during their bout with the war. Gerda and her family eventually made it back to the center in Wittenberge to the main street, which had changed names all throughout the war. Main Street had become Adolf Hitler Street and it was soon to return to Main Street. It was here that her heart sank as she saw the German soldiers in an unforgettable state.

Looking down the long, main drag of downtown Wittenberge, Gerda saw German soldiers of the Third Reich hanging from every tree on the street with their tattered, rag-covered feet dangling from their lifeless bodies. This was the punishment for those who deserted the orders of the Third Reich at this tenuous stage in the war. Instead of continuing to fight for Hitler, when there was overwhelming opposition from both the East and West, many of the German soldiers retreated, as the Suckows did. In turn, the German army executed these men for treason, usually by gunshot. Since the army lacked ammunition at this stage of war, they found other ways to kill the soldiers, such as by hanging. The swaying men haunted Gerda. She heard men speaking of deserters and saw what happened to them. The men deserted their mission because they had been defeated, not just militarily, but also their spirit. They were never given the resources to prosper and withheld the pride that was preached to them in the early stages of war. The country was now void of men, with boys as young as sixteen volunteering to fight for Germany. Gerda remembers such young boys committing seriously dangerous acts, like blowing up the main bridge into Wittenberge so no ally or foe could cross it.

One of Hitler's requirements of Germans was to contribute a few months of service to the country. Whether it was cleaning, or helping with farming, or assisting in any activity assigned, these tasks were mandated to make Germany a better place. Gerda's assignment had her at a farm, cleaning feces and maintaining a pigsty in Wittenberge. After living through years of ongoing war and carrying those smelly, stinking bodies, Gerda was not fazed by the gruesome task. During her time, one day, something truly amazing happened, something that could have changed the outlook on life for Gerda as well as bring an end to the war. During her service, she heard news that Hitler had been killed - or so she thought.

On July 20, 1944, a plan was set in motion to assassinate Adolf Hitler. A group of resistors had plotted to plant a briefcase that was to be detonated while Hitler was in a room for a meeting. One of Hitler's men accidentally kicked the briefcase to the side and the detonated bomb was deflected from Hitler, saving his life. After the failed attempt, the SA arrested 5,000 people, cleansing his own followers and military group of those that were plotting his downfall. Hitler's stronghold on Germany was diluting and this action was a symbol to intimidate resistors. Hitler's reach of terror knew no bounds, even at the cost of some of his own henchmen.

When Gerda was informed that someone tried to kill Hitler, she reacted with pure happiness. Gerda recalls how everyone was screaming in elation, thrilled with the notion that the grueling war was finally reaching its end. The natural emotion she felt was more of a relieved exultation. After all, she did not hate Hitler. In fact, she still revered him for giving her so much. She was still unaware of the horrible things he did, such as force people into labor camps and murder millions of innocent people. Gerda was not happy about the Third Reich falling. That would only leave the country in even more disarray. Gerda felt this relief because, to her, it meant that the war would be over. With Hitler's downfall, there would be no more bombing, no more rationing, no more living in fear wondering who would die next or if she would live the next day. Unfortunately, the attempted murder was thwarted, leaving Gerda with no clear indication of when the suffering would end.

Gerda was extremely upset by the destruction that the war brought to not only Wittenberge, but the many other cities in Germany that were also undeserving of the assault and devastation. Specifically, Gerda sadly recalls how Dresden was completely wiped out for no political reason whatsoever. Dresden was a city close to the Czechoslovakian border that was famed for its art and museums. It did not hold the same strategic weight as a city like Berlin. Regardless, the American and British troops also fire-bombed the city, reducing it to rubble and dust. With the Americans also capable of such devastation, Gerda felt she could not turn to anyone for help; not the Nazis, not God, and certainly not the Western and Eastern forces that were converging attacks on the town of Wittenberge. Instead, she stood alone, constantly running and avoiding the spinning attacks. Germany was relentlessly battling with all its neighboring countries at this point, and this signified the imminent possibility that the Nazi empire would soon crumble.

The most impressive and lasting military movement by the Western allied forces was led by General George S. Patton of the United States. With a small army, he moved swiftly through Germany, starting in 1943. Without much difficulty, he took over and occupied each territory he encountered. He continued to trek across central Europe, liberating each place he went. Suddenly German surrender seemed imminent, and he was ordered to stop. At one point, the American army occupied Wittenberge, which briefly put Gerda in a safe zone. But for a reason unknown to her, the American army left, and the Soviets came in. To Gerda and many other historians, Patton's brigade seemed so strong and determined that they could have marched all the way to Moscow if they so pleased. But Patton was ordered to fall back on his eastward bound movement, no longer acting as a continuously liberating force. By the time he reached the Czech Republic, the war was over. This was always frustrating to Gerda because she could have been spared much heartache and suffering had the United States stayed.

For Gerda, all of the bombings and intervention by Britain and America surely meant something. The forces from the West were getting stronger, and soon would be ready to overtake the Reich. These persistent threats, along with the diminishing strength of the German army, ultimately led to the death of Hitler by his own hand. On April 30, 1945, Hitler, feeling the pressure of complete domination from the Western forces, retreated with his wife to a bunker below Berlin. Both killed themselves: Hitler by gunshot and his wife Eva by ingesting a cyanide capsule. This time it was real. All the proclamations by the Third Reich that said Hitler's leadership would prosper for a thousand years were thwarted by a bullet and a pill. Hitler had long foreseen the end of his time on Earth and even had a pre-mandated list of instructions for what to do with his body. He ordered for his body to be cremated in the Chancellor's Garden. Like the many cities and people that were destroyed by Hitler, in some sense, he joined their state of dust and non-existence. With Hitler dying came more than just the end of a monstrous epoch. The state that he worked so hard to build by ruthless means was now left aloof, with all ideologies and promises unkept and destroyed.

To Gerda, it had finally come. The years of daily bombing, destruction and death now began to disintegrate. With no driving force behind the Third Reich, Hitler's movement was defeated. Many members of the Nazi party, including major leaders, would be subject to have their day in court and defend their inhumane actions. Others took the route of Hitler and avoided the suffering and embarrassment of warranted persecution by killing themselves. All of these men who swooned the hearts of their compatriots, manipulated their children into following extreme ideals, and committed unseen acts against humanity now showed their true colors in the face of justice: cowardly defeat and surrender. There was no honor or allegiance in this façade of an army - just selfishness and delusion.

Gerda had a similar feeling come over her, as she did when she was in the pigsty. She felt a sense of relief and happiness that her life would return to some sort of normalcy. This time, it was real. Hitler was dead. The country still stood in chaos and disorganization due to the years of destruction and radical political change. But that feeling inside Gerda of optimism and hope outweighed any apparent rubble. Now that Hitler was dead, the war would be over and all of her sufferings would seemingly begin to let up. This was the end of the bombs, the death, and the start of rebuilding her life and country, where she could once again be at ease and be a proud citizen. But there was a whole new set of problems and troubles that Gerda was to encounter that she was unaware of - experiences that would not overshadow the hardships of war, but again push her to the brink of hopelessness and change the course of her life forever.

Chapter Four

A NEW LOOK FOR WITTENBERGE AND EAST GERMANY (1945-1947)

As 1944 panned out into the New Year, although the battles of war were indeed intensifying to their highest peaks, the resistance against Hitler and Germany from the West was proving to be effective. The end of the war was drawing near. In February 1945, the Big Three met yet again in the South of the Ukraine, which would be known as the Yalta conference. During this conference, all parties recognized the imminent defeat of Nazism was clear. Stalin, Churchill, and Roosevelt met to decide how to deal with Germany as a post-war state. By this time, Russia had gone from being the victim to having the strongest military position of all Hitler's opposing forces. The leaders of their respective states decided preliminarily to divide Germany into four zones, where each state (including France) would have occupational control over their part of Germany to help rebuild and rectify the torn country into a self-sustaining, democratic nation. Since their political philosophies were so different, including a range from communism to democracy, the zone in which each German was residing would prove to be significant for Gerda and her fellow countrymen. When the war was over, in turn, the governing bodies of these assigned territories would adapt these philosophies.

With the death of Hitler came the rapid fall of the Third Reich, the prosperous state that was promised over the past decade. In reality, it translated to a gruesome war where death tolls tallied in unfathomable numbers by the most inhumane ways. Germany was now left without its chancellor and without the direction that was dictated by Hitler's master plan. Allied forces, which fought to end Hitler's monstrous tirade, were now moving to occupy the unsettled land in order to rebuild the destroyed nation of Germany. The Big Three met one last time to officially designate the zones of Germany at the Potsdam conference in July 1945. From one territory to the other, differences did not just exist with the bordered landscapes, but also in governing bodies, police, and laws.

At the Potsdam Conference, the plan to divide Germany into four zones was instituted: France, the United Kingdom, the United States, and the Soviet Union would each get a piece of the nation. The new era was most readily symbolized by the division of Berlin into two states by the Berlin wall, which designated one side the American zone and the other side the Soviet zone, each with their own respective ideals and demeanor. All powers involved in the decision agreed that such a division was the best way to keep peace among the different countries, as well as rectify all the damages and destruction from the years of war. Additionally and most importantly was the commitment to oversee the disassembly of the Third Reich and to destroy Nazism once and for all while holding those responsible for the actions of the movement accountable for their crimes against humanity and the destruction of Europe. Even though each nation had a similar agenda in approaching the reestablishment of Germany, their governments were not aligned in political philosophies or how they approached treating the German people.

From this point forward, Gerda's life would be identified with East Germany. Wittenberge was located in the zone just on the northern border of the Elbe River. The Soviet troops entered this zone and immediately began their administrative delegation of this section of Germany. Gerda did not anticipate how the Soviet soldiers would act or how she would be treated. She was happy to no longer be face to face with daily bombings and death, but the country that remained after all the destruction seemed bleak and unsettled. There was an undeniable sense of uneasiness about where things would go and how the state would be organized, how the city would be rebuilt, and a myriad of other matters. Gerda never understood why the Americans had left. Unluckily, Wittenberge was geographically set in a zone that was not free from harm. For that, the hardships were to continue. Now, she found herself in a unique position with a new government, lost identity, and an ambiguous future that nobody could predict.

Following the Potsdam conference, the Soviet-occupied zone instituted the Socialist Unity Party of Germany known as the SED. A Red Army was established through the state to enforce the laws with the party acting as the government. The German people had just finished dealing with the Nazi party, who instilled their ideals and forced people to join it. Now, there was a new occupation, and the people had to accept an entirely new set of values and ideals that were being thrust upon them. For many people, switching so radically to a new lifestyle and philosophy was troubling enough considering all they went through in the recent years of the war. Generally, many people view the Germans as ready participants in Nazism and torment during World War II, but the truth is that many of its people were simply going along with what was happening to avoid persecution and arrest. Many of the German people were unaware to the severe extent of the death camps during the years of war, and were, in a way, just as ignorant as the people around the world who were removed from what was truly happening. Now, East Germans were presented with a new enforcing body that came with a chip on its shoulder, with the Russians seeking reparations from their own hardships during World War II. Gerda, still elated by the end of the war, took time to adjust to these motives from her new acting government.

Coming off a betrayal that cost the country many lives, a newly-empowered Stalin led the begrudged Soviets against Germany. The Soviet Union was initially defeated by the German forces that infiltrated their state earlier in the war, and never had the plentiful or modern resources that other major powers possessed. The soldiers fought blindly and loyally on a daily basis without any time for leave or break. Most of the time they were being outmatched or outnumbered. Part of the Potsdam Conference dictated that each zone would also be granted payment for damages during the War. For the Soviet Union, this was especially important. They did not have much to begin with, and the soldiers suffered a lonely and devastating time during the war. Germany was not in the best of shape, either. Stalin and his subjects did not use this opportunity to just help Germany, but also to further the prosperity of their own state by absorbing resources from East Germany and taking advantage of her people.

A NEW LOOK FOR WITTENBERGE AND EAST GERMANY (1945-1947)

When Gerda first encountered the newly-appointed Soviet occupation, she was standing with her father as the Red Army rode downtown. A group of Soviet troops on horseback trotted toward them, and asked if Gerda and her father knew the time. When they looked down at their watches, the soldiers took the timepieces off their wrists with no hesitation, and rode away. This was an indication of how Gerda's life was destined to be for the following years under the occupation of the Soviet Union. Gerda and her father stood on the street, perplexed not at the actions of the soldier, but at the thought that the new government would not carry much improvement. Nazism was over and Hitler was dead, but there was a new breed of evil that they were about to encounter, one that was politically assigned by some of the most powerful forces in the world to govern their state. The Soviet soldiers fought for Stalin during Gerda's entire war experience without getting the privilege or break to see their families, or do anything outside of following orders and engaging in battles and purges, which led them to be curt and even brutal.

To Gerda, the soldiers were sad and stupid. They seemed like an ignorant breed of simple folk who did not show any signs of intuition or deep thought. Gerda looked at these men as the foot soldiers they were. They were not being compassionate to the victims of a people who just endured a depleting war, but rather halfheartedly and leisurely made their presence in this new state convincingly known. Although Germany was not completely taken over by these occupying troops, the Soviets were the overseeing and enforcing body in her town. With the uncertainty this new group brought, Gerda quickly realized that she was unlucky to be on this side of Germany after the war. The Americans and British from the West were implementing a democratic system and rebuilding Germany with valor and independence. On the Eastern side, they instituted the communist rule that Gerda had been conditioned to oppose from her days in the Hitler Youth. The differences from where Gerda lived and the West were not just ideological, but the tactics used by the Soviets were cruder and more severe.

The dissolution of the Third Reich allowed for the freedom of imprisoned laborers from concentration camps and other German prisons. These refugees were released back into the world, many times without knowing where their family was, or if they were alive. At Potsdam, the Big Three meted out justice for Germany as well as its inherent refugees from Hitler's persecutions throughout Europe. Almost all native Germans who had not been ousted by the SA were required to

40

house a number of refugees who were dislocated from the war. The Suckows were assigned a young Lithuanian girl and her mother, who stayed in their family's home after the war. That was also when the Soviet soldiers began their surge of rape in Wittenberge.

Since the Red Army's soldiers were not allowed to visit their families during the war's climax, reaching its apex when Hitler died in 1945, Red Army comrades essentially ordered for its men to do as they pleased with the women in what was now East Germany. This mandate led to one of the most infamous surges of abuse and rape the world may have ever seen, leaving the women in Germany vulnerable and prone. With nobody to regulate, the Soviet soldiers would commit these crimes against females as young as two years old, and as old as eighty, with no discretion or humility in the actions they were to carry out. Even though the war ended in 1945, there was no clue to the state of fear of being abused that Gerda experienced following the end of what should have been the most trying experience of her life.

The horrors that followed these actions were perhaps even worse then imagined. For example, Gerda tells how the German soldiers would take their blades to the vaginas of little girls, who could not even ride a bicycle, in order to fit their penises inside them, putting an end to their innocence and even their life. It became almost a game to these soldiers, who had not felt a woman's touch in their service to Stalin. They took every opportunity they could to exploit any German girl they felt like victimizing. They were the ones with the power and the weapons to enable these activities and there was not much anyone could do to stop it. Irresponsible with power, many of the militants would do as they pleased with whomever they encountered, whether it was a playful mass execution or the abuse and rape of local women. The Soviet soldiers who acted in this manner did not see value in the German's lives, but rather toyed with them in the most fatal and pervasive of ways. Germans became so terrified by the constant raping that they began to report each other to avoid being raped, willingly sacrificing others for their own safety. Some girls were even raped dozens of times in separate incidents. The sense of community and quaint livelihood in Wittenberge was shattered by the rampant acts of rape and murder. Gerda could not help but question not only when this would all end, but why it was happening to her.

The Russian soldiers entered Germany with the motivation of retribution for the sufferings they endured during the war, even if that was not the intention delegated by the Potsdam conference. The Soviet soldiers were on a power trip of epic proportion, drinking heavily and relying only on primal feelings of lust and anger. They used the women as an outlet and had no apparent sympathy. To Gerda, these men always had a knife in their boot, and were ready to kill. Under the influence of a communist state, Gerda encountered a new type of evil and it drove her to a darker state of mind than during the war. Seeing death come from above during the war left her with an emptiness and lack of hope, while this new feeling of victimization brought her to a state of both fear and enmity. Never in her life had she wanted to kill someone, but the way that these communists were acting and conducting themselves planted the seed of hate inside of her. She began to feel the fire inside her grow, more than she had ever imagined she could hate anyone in her life up to this very moment.

Living in this state, where opposition was surely a losing cause, the only seemingly viable option was escape. One of Gerda's childhood friends tried to escape from the terror by train. She had enough of living in a Germany that was controlled and overseen by the communists. Fed up with the brutality, she went by railroad to escape to West Germany, away from Russian occupation. Unfortunately, her plan was thwarted by the Soviets, who found her and a few other girls hidden in the back of a boxcar. With nowhere to run to, the girls were each raped by the Soviet soldiers. Gerda heard that they had been sliced to pieces after being raped. The heaviness of the news was devastating. Whether the crimes committed were happening to strangers or friends, these stories intimidated Gerda and her family. Escape seemed too risky.

Gerda's father decided to take action to protect the young women of his household. Running away was a poor option because the risk of getting caught was very high and the penalty would be at the mercy of the soldiers who would catch them. The only other option was to hide, but with Germans reporting each other to save themselves, there was not much security in staying at home. So Otto, the handyman, built a secret room in the attic of their chicken coupe, located in the back of the house. He constructed a set of dummy walls with a hidden trap door allowing passage when needed. There was enough room for only a few people. From the outside, someone who climbed the ladder to the attic would see a wall, but it was actually one side of the safe room that Otto had built. Otto and Gerda determined this was the best plan of action to insure that they would remain untouched by the Soviet soldiers.

The Lithuanian girl and Gerda would stay in the hideaway for nearly all their time in the following six months, except for when they had to use the bathroom or occasionally clean the house. Otto cooked them meals and delivered food to them through a small trap door he had made that flapped in a small section of the floor. As young, pretty and untouched girls, Gerda and the refugee would have been the desired victims for the Soviet soldiers. Gerda and her new housemate sat quietly most of the time, trying to read and keep themselves preoccupied from the notion that at most times Soviets were looking for girls to rape and abuse. The girls felt a sense of security in the attic, but the realization that at any moment the small door could be opened, the dummy wall knocked down, and then the SED could capture them loomed.

At times, the SED would knock on the Suckows door claiming other Germans told them that girls lived in the house. On these occasions, Gerda had to remain perfectly still, muffling her breathing to the slightest murmur, so as not to be detected by the SED. The tenuous moments felt like years to the girls, and were some of the most anxious of Gerda's life. At a time when praying may have been an appropriate outlet, Gerda still felt the void of God in her as she thought back at the horrors she already endured. What had happened? She was ready to become a chemist, training to swim at the Olympics, singing songs and marching with friends. Now, she was reduced to cowering in a corner, with no faith or hope in her that things would get better. The only reality was the fear of being brutalized. As Gerda spent more time alone in the attic, she went to a darker place that was truly introspective and scary.

Gerda spent nearly six months perched in the attic, anxiously hiding from the Soviet soldiers. Otto's plan was a success, as Gerda and the Lithuanian girl remained safe in the hideaway. Over the course of the six months, the Soviet soldiers slowed their victimization of the women of East Germany, and began to carry out new orders. Stalin was receiving criticism for the actions of his Red Army. He fought back in the press saying that these vulgar actions of the Red Army were defaming his state and what they stood for. He then ordered for the rape and abuse to cease and it did slow down. East Germany was still left as rubble and the rebuilding and reorganization of the state had not gotten off the ground. In an effort to kick-start this process, nearly all citizens would help clean up. Gerda collected bricks around Wittenberge, where she would then clean the cement off them to be used in new buildings and homes.

Gerda helped clean around the rayon factory in town where she once worked as an apprentice. The building that once harbored the sculpting of her dreams to become a chemist now stood as a shell, destroyed from the war. The newly appointed Soviet army would disgrace it even further. Gerda witnessed the SED stealing the faucets and light fixtures from inside the factory. The soldiers saw light coming from the bulbs, so they thought that was where electricity came from. They took the faucets because that is where they saw water come from. They would even wash their heads in the toilets because there was running water. It was amazing to Gerda how dumb these men really were. They knew nothing about science or the workings of the world outside of their communist teachings and orders from senior officers. They were told to take everything, and that is just what they did.

In light of all the terrible things that the SED was doing and seeing their stupidity in action, Gerda gained a unique opinion about these men. She most certainly had negative feelings toward them, and hated the truly cruel ones. But, there was an even purer feeling deep inside of her that is difficult to comprehend. She pitied them. She felt sorry for them. Even though they committed horrific crimes, she ultimately did not find them at fault, for they were the victims of their own hardships. She understood that they had a terrible experience with war surrounded by nothing but death and other sad men. Gerda sympathized with their pain and could see, no matter how hard it was, that they were just sad, pathetic people with no opportunity outside what was given. Her unique perspective viewed these soldiers having nothing but a bleak future and a mindset that was clearly tainted by the extreme ideals of their communist leader.

In a way, Gerda and these men shared a similar experience. Gerda led a life evaluated by someone who she only later recognized as illogical and radical. She also followed orders blindly and thought she was doing what was right. After all, at one time she even subjected her own father to persecution and other punishment, something that now seemed unthinkable. The SED, too, were caught up in this war where reality, clarity, and a normal life were completely irrelevant. They could only work with what was available and move within the unique parameters set by the ever-changing government and hostile climate of Eastern Europe. Suddenly it seemed both Gerda and the soldiers, along with the others in Wittenberge, became one state under dire circumstances.

Chapter Five

ASSIMILATING UNDER SOVIET RULE
(1947-1949)

With the unlucky reality of Wittenberge being geographically set in the Soviet zone of the newly divided Germany, Gerda and her family had to adjust to a new kind of lifestyle. This always confused Gerda as a child. Technically and politically, this was the correct move. Splitting the zones into distinct sections was intended to limit aggression between the West and East. But, in carving up the territory for political purposes, they compromised and changed the lives of the people who originally lived there.

The Soviet soldiers always seemed a bit dim-witted to Gerda. She would ride her bicycle into town and get stopped by the SED, who would then steal it from her. Later on, the very same laborers that she brought sandwiches to prior to the Soviet occupation would give her a bicycle in return as appreciation for taking care of them in a time of need. Although these good deeds were a symbol of some compassion, the SED would then steal the bicycles back as soon as they met Gerda again. To Gerda, It became a hilarious merry-go-round of give-and-take for her and her friend. They would get a bicycle, and then get it taken away. Get a bike taken away, then given a different one. She thought the soldiers were so stupid, and could not help but laugh at their actions even if they were in good spirit.

Although she was not planning any resistance or causing any stir, Gerda, like many Germans, were suspected by the SED of being spies for the West, and plotting against the Soviets. Gerda's first arrest was due to her contact with family members in other parts of Germany. Simply keeping in contact with people outside of Wittenberge was enough reason for the SED to have reason to arrest and interrogate someone. Six Soviet soldiers first approached Gerda, standing tough with their bayonettes in hand. They took her from her home and led her into a limousine for interrogation. Six men for just one person seems like an arrest for an awfully serious allegation, but it was not. Not only was this the first time she had ever been arrested, but this was also Gerda's first time being in a car. Her family never owned an automobile, much less traveled inside one for any reason. Gerda's first privilege to ride in the innovative machine came under duress. Stoic in the situation, she did not resist nor fight against being arrested. They brought her to the basement of City Hall and interrogated her about being a spy. They asked her in every way possible if she had an affiliation with the West, or any intentions to bring down or conspire against the SED. Gerda did not have anything to hide and was honest with the soldiers. Before long, they let her go. This became a common theme in East Germany – frequent arrests.

Once Stalin ordered the SED to curtail their surge of violence and rape against the German people, the newly-ruled zone including Wittenberge began to move toward a postwar state. Rationing continued, as the free market was not fully functional so soon after the chaos. This action further advocated socialist ideals, ones that put government-sanctioned actions as priorities over an individual's free will. In fact, through each phase of Gerda's life, she never experienced a time where there was not at least some rationing of goods. Just like during the war, Gerda was again forced to wait in line in order to get food to eat and cigarettes to smoke. The Soviets served boiled potato sandwiches, just plainly-sliced boiled potatoes between two pieces of bread, every day. At the time, this tasted like cake to Gerda, as it was the only form of sustenance readily available. Gerda had not been to a proper restaurant in the previous nine years and that streak continued with the informality of businesses and jobs being regulated by the Soviets, with no true ownership. Additionally, few people had money to spend and were trying to assimilate to the new ways of life in Wittenberge, one that did not reflect the traditional pastimes before World War II.

Gerda's mother began to work as a seamstress for the Russians, sewing the Soviet army's uniforms as things began to calm down. The soldiers wore old and faded uniforms, as Russia lacked finances during the war. Their equipment, artillery, and apparel were not up to the standards of neighboring countries, and the Soviet state felt they were owed reparations for these inadequacies. This spurred the soldiers to essentially strip the factories and industries of East Germany, and bring the newly-acquired amenities to Russia. They took everything from the factories, which left them vacant buildings with no hope of reopening the businesses. The rayon factory where Gerda once worked now stood as a brick building with nothing inside. The byproduct from this factory was molasses, which was given to Gerda's mother in exchange for her services as a seamstress.

The Soviets always watched Minna sew the cloth in a way that was eerie to Gerda. She could not tell if they were fascinated or eyeing her mother with thoughts of rape. With the buckets of molasses, Minna would feed Gerda and her family, creating a change of pace to the predictable boiled potato sandwiches they had grown accustomed to. Gerda remembers working at the factory and having to smell the pungent odor of the molasses. The scent was unavoidable but she endured the smell because it was simply a characteristic of her job. However, now it became one of her primary sources for food. How the barely sufficient fare represented the ceiling of opportunity for Gerda, or how it was a meal of desperation, not indulgence, was not a controversial thought for the family. Even though the war was over, more struggles and hardships were imminent.

Minna was not the only member of the family finding some opportunity, or at least as much that was possible, in the Soviet zone of Germany. Gerda's sister Hannelore had adapted to her new surroundings as well. From childhood, Hannelore and Gerda took slightly different paths. Gerda got her scholarship and went to study chemistry. Hannelore, on the other hand, was not granted the same opportunity. They ran in different circles and did not have the same group of friends. Where Gerda had camaraderie with her swim team and the Hitler Youth, Hannelore had a different set of friendships and led a more independent lifestyle.

As a child, Gerda would try to include her sister in activities and invite her to other events with friends. But, Hannelore always had some excuse not to go, whether it was not feeling well, feeling left out, or simply not wanting to. Hannelore was always the type who liked to walk alone, feeling disjointed from the expected habits of her peers. She had her

47

own intimate experience and introspection within the years of war, which led her to apply for a job with the SED as an officer. Becoming an officer in this new state was not necessarily a move of surrender or complacency. It is what was necessary in order to live. Although Hannelore had some ulterior motives in taking this position, Gerda decided that maybe it was time for her to start working as well. She was no longer living in the attic of the chicken coupe, and escaping East Germany was not a wise or viable option at the time. As long as she was in this unfortunate position, she may as well make the best of it, Gerda thought.

Gerda saw an advertisement for a teaching position and took it. It had been a few years since Gerda was involved with a school system, a pastime that she always loved but could not continue due to the hectic events of the war. She inquired about the position and given her previous education and experience was granted the opportunity. The process of being a teacher was not as exclusive as it had been when Gerda was a student in Wittenberge. Under Hitler, teachers were required to have a PhD, whereas Gerda did not even get to complete her time in school. Before she began her training as a teacher, Gerda was arrested for a second time. This interrogation was very similar to her first arrest and was most likely a precursor to her employment through the government. Clearly, she was not a serious person of interest. The Russians trained Gerda to be a teacher in less than eight months. She began working immediately after her release.

To Gerda it was laughable how short the period of time was to train to be a teacher and learn the curriculum of such a job. She wondered if someone could learn anything in such a short amount of time. There was one subject that Gerda was not permitted to teach, something that was not a part of the courses included for the children: German history. Ingeniously, the Russians decided that such a current topic would not be useful in the reshaping of the new East Germany under Soviet occupation. She was not allowed to teach this because for the Russians who would be her students, such material was not yet relevant in their lives. There was also some fear about what Gerda might have said to the kids, as a German herself. She was arrested for a third time during her training. By this point, she became familiar with the procedures for these arrests, and was more annoyed than fearful about these imprisonments. They did not have her in harsh conditions or brutalize her like some other spies experienced. Instead, her captors were relentless in their inquisition. It could not have been too serious of an allegation against

Gerda, being that at no point had they dismissed her for becoming a teacher.

After she finished her training, Gerda was assigned to teach Russians in the third and fourth grades in the countryside outside Wittenberge. When first approaching the facility where she would be teaching, Gerda was surprised at how big the compound was, surrounded by metal gates. It appeared to be a castle from the outside, like she was going to be teaching for royalty. Her guesses were somewhat validated, as this was a place where a sort of royalty had once convened. The new school was at the hunting compound of Hermann Goering, the Nazi leader of the SA. At one point in time, this is where Goering, Hitler, and many other influential members of the Nazi party would retreat to discuss plans, decompress, or go hunting. Like Hitler, Goering sealed his own fate by suicide. This compound, which not too long ago hosted retreats for some of the most incorrigibly evil and calculating men from the Third Reich, became a school for Russian children in East Germany. It is very possible that the kids that Gerda was assigned to teach were children of relatively essential members of the newly placed SED. In an oddly similar circumstance, Gerda was once in this position under the guise of the Hitler Youth, and now provided similar training for the Soviets. The SED was placed to end Nazism and change the culture of East Germany. Ironically, they were taking the form of the very people they were replacing. Even though the Nazis and socialists differed in philosophy, the control and execution of these values were quite similar.

Gerda enjoyed teaching thoroughly, partly because she was good at it but also because such an occupation located outside the major city was a way of being set apart from the chaos of the reestablishment of Germany. Gerda kept in touch with her family, not just in Wittenberge, but other parts of Germany through mail and packages, keeping tabs of everyone's wellbeing and assimilation into the Soviet lifestyle. This was not just a new government, but a new party, and in communism, a new ideal being imparted on the German people. Some were receptive to the idea, and went along with the higher powers to avoid persecution. But others were more hesitant to follow this new philosophy, given the poor experience with the Nazi party during World War II. Gerda did not seek to join *any* sort of party. At the time, she was content with her station, which had her seemingly out of harm's way, in the woods teaching at Goering's former compound. Even though the Soviets were employing Germans and the rape and violence tapered off, the harshness of their rule came hand in hand with a series of arrests and interrogations to ensure that their agenda was not thwarted or compromised.

After her first few months of teaching, Gerda was arrested for a fourth time. Unlike the previous three, this detention was not routine. This was a result of a certain group of people who at one point in time were close friends with Gerda. The SED gained some peculiar interest in a riveting investigation that had even Gerda a bit shocked. Many of the kids Gerda knew from the Hitler Youth to her time as a teacher were in serious trouble with the SED for a plotted attack on the Soviet Army headquarters in Wittenberge, better known as the Komnandantur. It was not unwarranted suspicions that led the SED to think Gerda played some role in this plan. Through their interrogations, the SED must have learned that Gerda and the assailants were tied together as close friends for years. Gerda was held for nearly a week as the SED questioned her about all her ties to the militia group and other parties involved. The SED found radio equipment and other materials above City Hall that were used to contact West Germany in a plot to take down the SED headquarters in Wittenberge. Gerda soon realized that this was legitimate, that stakes were high for the SED and her involvement was reasonably questionable.

Gerda, however, did not have any knowledge of this operation. She was purposely not informed of the activities of the rogue group because her father's best friend was a commissioned driver for the SED, and they feared she might leak information. Like the other times Gerda was arrested, the SED found no convincing evidence or indication that would lead them to think she was involved, as much as she may have wanted to. Being excluded from this operation saved Gerda's life, but it did not fill the void inside her.

Although Gerda was far removed from Wittenberge teaching in the woods, the events in the war and the trauma she had experienced were always fresh in her mind. There was that burning hate inside her toward those who caused these events to transpire and through that feeling she always wanted some opportunity to fight, to stand for herself. Being so removed had skewed her perceptions about what was still happening in Wittenberge. She was no longer living there, but hearing about its battles. It made her want to take action. Gerda thought about her most recent history with the Soviets. She remembers vividly hiding from the soldiers in her chicken coupe, and also watching her workplace getting stripped and destroyed. Gerda had a yearning to be atoned for her troubles. This was not necessarily a vindictive feeling, but more of unresolved justice.

At the time, Gerda was upset that she could not be a part of the coup, with all of her angst and frustration toward the Soviet soldiers who abused, stole, and took advantage of the German people. However, being left out of the plan may have been a blessing in disguise. All of the members of this small group were arrested and not just interrogated or imprisoned, but executed. Her friends, although rightfully motivated, paid the ultimate price for their actions. By not being told the contents of this operation, Gerda's life was spared and she was able to return to her job as a teacher as if nothing happened at all. But Gerda was not fully excluded from the drama and potential dangers of the militant activities in Wittenberge, even being so far secluded while teaching outside town. No matter where she was, or what job she had, or how normal life may have seemed out in the countryside, she was still under Soviet occupation and not content with her station in life.

Gerda embraced her job as a teacher, imparting whatever knowledge she could to the Russian children. Given her unique position and conditions, she genuinely loved helping the young students. She identified with their innocence and ambition. She saw a bit of herself in the impressionable youth who were being raised in a lifestyle under communism, one that Gerda became accustomed to, but did not choose to accept. It was not like the Hitler Youth, where she and all her friends were unwillingly brought into it. Joining the SED was something that Gerda had a choice in. The Soviet zone was built under the preconception that they were going to reestablish a democracy in their respective zones, rather than simply rule and dictate like it was a conquered territory. The Soviets took advantage of this pact and the country's people, especially the women. Gerda was always pressured into joining the SED, but it simply was not for her. She was forced into a party once before, and the results were anything but favorable. She did not want to take a chance on a system that she did not believe in.

Gerda's refusal did not come without a cost. Even though she was quite good at teaching, she was going to be fired for resisting to join the SED. Although she found relative happiness in her position, the Soviets once again would take away a part of her life due to her reluctance to reform. Before her time was up, she decided that she would teach the Russians a lesson, one that the SED could not do anything about. She wanted to leave a lasting impression on the children, even if they did not realize the impact of what they were learning at the time. She taught them a German song called "Die Gedanken Sind Frei" that was

51

originally created as a protest against the Nazi party. As the whole class sang together, she listened contently to the tune that was once her outlet against the ruling government during a war she could not control. In this instance, though the target was different, she was able to teach it to them maintaining the essence of the ballad. The main message of the song is "The thoughts are free. Who can guess them?" This intends to say that nobody can take away your thoughts and nobody can see what you think inside your head. It is the one place that no matter the situation, you are free to think as you please. Reflecting into Gerda's past, she recalls the tumultuous moments where everything was tense around her. It is at these times where she wanted to impart to the children that they can own their thoughts, think positively, and be free.

One day, while teaching, Gerda's lesson was interrupted by soldiers of the SED, who arrested her one last time. She would inevitably be fired, but first she was placed under arrest. Gerda was taken to a prison in Potsdam, located just a few hours outside her hometown of Wittenberge. From the moment she stepped out of the car onto the grounds, she knew something was different about this arrest. This was not simply a routine or useless interrogation in the bottom of City Hall. In this place, she felt fear creeping inside her, when usually she would be stoically numb in such a situation. This was a prison, a *real* prison. The guards forcefully pushed her through the main doors, poking at her back as they led her up the metal stairs. Approaching one of the cells, Gerda was more frightened than she had ever been. There was metal all around her, from the floors to the walls, to the bars that slammed shut on the cell that she would share with others. The guards shoved her inside her cell, and she stumbled onto the cold moist floor. Once the cell door clicked in, the reality of her current situation was clear: this was not going to be easy.

As Gerda's hands pushed her up from the floor, she peered around inside the dim cell. It looked dark and bleak. The floor felt dirty, accented by the filthy, lifeless and sullen faces that looked at her with a sense of pity and lasting sadness. She shared her cell with two German girls and one American girl in the prison. The three tired and dirty girls were standing, staring at Gerda with a look of sympathy and regret as she was pushed into the cell. They had been imprisoned for a while, and it showed. Gerda looked around the cell and saw two bunk beds, where she would inevitably sleep. She could not believe the awful stench coming from the corner. There was a large bowl, bigger than a toilet that was split in half with no drains coming into or out of it. Piling from the half-round bowl was disregarded, stinking excrement and stale urine. This was to be their bathroom, and there was nowhere for the waste to go or a sense of privacy. It stunk to high heaven and added another odor to Gerda's list of unpleasant smells that came with hardship, just like the stink of burning bodies during the war.

Gerda quickly learned that prisoners were not allowed to sit, which is why the girls constantly remained standing. Unpredictable punishment awaited anyone who was caught sitting or resting. Sometimes it could be a simple reprimand, and at other times, it could be more severe or abusive. On one occasion, her German cellmate was caught sitting, and a guard ordered her to face the wall kneeling down. She had to stay this way for hours on end, and cried the entire time. Gerda remembers the hours of non-stop weeping from the pain, humiliation, and helplessness that the girl was feeling. Gerda tried kneeling as well, to see what it felt like and cowered in pain within minutes. Already weak, malnourished, and lacking rest, this position was difficult to endure.

The girls were in constant silence during their time in Potsdam. They were never allowed to speak to each other for fear of further punishment. Gerda once again felt as if there was no hope for her. She was sure this was the place where she would die. Between the murky atmosphere and the uneasy vibes throughout the prison, Gerda did not see any light to the darkness that surrounded her. The two German girls were in situations similar to Gerda. They were taken from their newly adapted life, and accused of espionage. The American girl, however, was in a unique position. She was caught with an American soldier in East Germany, and sent to Potsdam in secret. No one was permitted or allowed to know where she was. Gerda never found out what came of that girl, but it is unlikely that she was released. To the Soviets, she represented the Western front, where all the spies' allegiances lied.

At the prison, meals were also irregular or sparingly granted. The guards would unreliably come by at different times, sometimes days elapsing before the next meal, sliding a metal tray into the cell. Gerda ate the leftover stumps from cabbages that were boiled earlier. Each girl was given one trunk. If it was not the restlessness or the foul stench, then it was the hunger that started to play tricks with the girls' heads. Surrounded by steel, with nothing to eat, and no one to speak to, Gerda's hopelessness had her wondering why this place existed and even further, why she deserved to be there. She had been arrested many times before, always to be interrogated, but never like this.

The interrogations were held every single night, never during the day. After a long day of standing in silence in the putrid cell, the guards would take each girl to be interrogated and questioned separately. Gerda would be led barefoot down the metal stairs as the guards kicked the back of her heels with their steel-toed boots. Every prisoner at Potsdam appeared to have the same bloody heels. There was no glimpse of compassion from any of the SED in Potsdam. One time, a girl had her period inside the cell and a guard managed the situation by tearing a piece of wool from a nearby blanket. This same cruel treatment carried into every encounter during her time in Potsdam.

The interrogations became a blur after a while. All night the guards screamed at Gerda and the already suffering and weak inmates, asking if they were spies, or whom they worked for, or if they had any information. Even though her responses never yielded anything of interest, the guards were relentless in their pursuit, repetitively drilling the same questions into the dazed and exhausted girl without any difference in response. By this point in her life, Gerda had been through much trauma, but she never grew to hate people like she did these guards. She especially despised the women, who were significantly meaner than the men. If there was any time in her life where she felt like killing someone, this was it. To Gerda, these people had no heart or soul, and deserved to die for the way they treated the inmates. The Nazis, who had been working at the labor and concentration camps, may have deserved such treatment to reciprocate for their cruel actions, but Gerda was not one of them. None of her actions had ever warranted this treatment. She was just a girl who got a scholarship to school, excelled at swimming, and followed the rules. But it was only to end up in a place like this. She was ready to die.

An act that was enforced in Germany said that a person could not be imprisoned longer than twenty-seven days without a legitimate reason. The SED kept her there for the entirety of that period. During her time at Potsdam, she never had a break from interrogation, or time to rest. After being tortured and tormented in such a way for so long, days lost their meaning, as did time. And it was not just Gerda. All the others who were in the cells, who were there before, and who would be taken there under arrest in the future would suffer the same fate. What would happen to these people? Thinking of this was truly depressing for Gerda. Any life that entered into those stinking cells would amount to the broken person she was. Life became what existed within the metal walls of Potsdam. Nothing else made sense to Gerda. She was successfully taken out of the world and put into a place where faith was as worthless as it was years back, when carrying all those bodies.

Gerda spent exactly twenty-seven days in Potsdam. She was released without much notice, as if a bell had rung and that was that. They opened the gates after leading her outside and she began to run. Disoriented, she had no idea where she was going, or what she was going to do, but she just continued to run and run. In such a fragile state of mind, Gerda did not recall how she made it home. It was never clear why exactly Gerda was arrested this time around. Whether it was because of her refusal to join the communist party or general suspicion of espionage, Gerda no longer wanted to preoccupy herself with these thoughts. She was away from it finally, and that was good enough. After enduring such duress and mental molestation, she was in no condition to understand how to perceive reality as anything but empty. All she knew was that she could not continue to live like this anymore. She did not want to spend all of her days anticipating arrest and waiting for the Soviets to make their next move in a state of constant confrontation, anxiety and vapid hope. She vowed never to spend another day in prison, committed to escape East Germany or die trying: an ultimatum that, to her, was fortuitous in either result.

Hannelore, Minna, Otto and Gerda Suckow, 1949

Chapter Six

ESCAPING EAST GERMANY (1949)

After being released from prison, Gerda somehow made it back to her parent's home in Wittenberge. The torturous conditions that she endured would haunt her forever, even if she could not recall every specific moment of her time in those cold walls. Gerda was extremely disoriented and malnourished, resulting in a blur of memories and a shaky state of mind. Gerda was now committed to escape this life that she had grown to despise. She did not even attempt to return to the school, where she knew she would be fired. She did not contact any friends to confide in and share her traumatic experience, or even say goodbye. Instead, she went home to her mother.

Although Minna was not usually demonstratively affectionate, she reacted to Gerda's story with the desire to protect her child. Gerda shared her experience and basic feelings, expressing her need to leave forever, and finally begin heading to America. Determined, the two decided to find a way for Gerda to escape East Germany to the West, and send her away from the Soviets to a place under British and American occupation. There, abuse and arrest were not happening like they were under the Soviets. Gerda's mother took it upon herself to lead the quest for her daughter's safety, no matter the cost.

Minna decided that they had to be very careful. After all, they all knew of many people who tried to do the same thing and ended up caught and suffered devastating consequences. Gerda no longer feared death or capture. Above all, the continuation of pain and suffering scared her the most. Minna collected all the money that she could. She even included some West German notes, to give to Gerda so if she were to successfully leave East Germany, she would have some footing in her new life. To secure Gerda's escape, Minna approached a German who had become a soldier for the SED. There were a few other people who also approached the same man. They talked of a boat that would cross the Elbe River to the other side of Germany, outside of Soviet occupation. This sounded like the best option. Gerda remembered the tragedy that her friends endured in their attempt to leave by train. Traveling by bicycle was not an option, either. The trek would be too long and too dangerous to risk getting caught.

Gerda met the guard with a small bag of belongings, and said goodbye to her family. Leaving them, she knew it might be the last time she would see them, or Wittenberge, ever again. Hannelore would go on to work as a policewoman for the SED while her parents would stay in Wittenberge. Fleeing was the right decision for Gerda, who had already been through so much. This would bring her one step closer to her dream of getting to America. Just like the stories she read of Heidi as a little girl, Gerda, too, was going to America. First, she had to cross the Elbe River.

A small boat was docked for her and around ten other hopeful men and women. They all eagerly awaited their own chance to permanently escape from East Germany. The group loaded into the boat and prepared to set across the Elbe River. The boat set off, and for a moment Gerda felt a sensation that she had not even thought of in years: relief. However, this was to be short-lived, as the boat was intercepted almost immediately by Soviet troops. Their plan was thwarted from the very start. The man schemed to collect money from all these people hoping to escape a life under Soviet rule, and made little effort to make the trip successful, keeping the profits regardless. The Soviet troops herded the dozen or so Germans from the boat like cattle being grazed into pasture. Gerda was arrested yet again.

At this point, Gerda was not surprised. She sulked, barely having the energy or strength to act animated. Looking back, she should have been furious, frustrated, screaming for her life and freedom. At that moment, she only felt defeated. Her chance at escape was foiled. Everything in her life seemed to build toward something good, only to have it taken away or ruined. Like her dreams of being a chemist or swimming in the Olympics, this too was put out of reach due to politics and boundaries beyond her control. The troops brought Gerda and the others to a cramped makeshift containment area. The Soviet soldiers seemed confused about how to deal with these attempted escapees. They no longer maimed or raped the German people, and seemed interested in more pressing issues to Gerda. All the while, Gerda did not care. In that moment, she lost the passion for living and, once again, her sense of faith. The only hope she saw for herself existed on the other side of the Elbe River in West Germany. Here, she had nothing.

Shortly after they were intercepted, Gerda and the others were released from the holding cell. Gerda, once again deflated, returned to her family. Gerda continued to feel she had no place in Wittenberge. The town made her think of those days in Potsdam and memories of the war. She weighed all her options for another escape attempt. She was struggling to come up with a way to cross the river without getting caught. If she were to go by boat, evidently that would be too visible and she would get caught yet again. That left only one way to get across that river. It was something that she had been doing all her life, a hobby that once led her to different countries and for this time, a last resort to salvation.

In March 1949, at twenty-one years old, Gerda was going to swim across the Elbe River through the blistering cold of a German winter. Based on the extremely low temperature of the water alone, death was a very realistic possibility. In addition, there were many other dangers involved including colliding with other watercrafts and of course, capture. Gerda once again said goodbye to her family. This time, she had no intention of coming back at all. She was prepared to die during this last attempt at escape and relative freedom from the imprisoned and limited life she had in a communist Wittenberge.

Gerda approached the barbed wire gates that bordered the Elbe River. Although the conditions were a bit more dangerous, she decided to go at night, in order to limit the potential of being seen or getting caught. Soviet soldiers were always guarding the river since it was the border of East and West Germany. Gerda laid low, carefully watching how the soldiers would march. Eventually, she noticed a pattern that would spark a strategy for escape. The soldiers would be working in pairs, marching toward each other, meeting in the center, then turning around and marching away from each other to the ends of their designated areas. They would repeat this motion with precision, continuously singing and marching all the way. From the time the Soviets first moved into Wittenberge, Gerda had always noticed that they were marvelous singers. They would chant in unison during their marches in a way that she could not help but perceive as beautiful. For a brief moment, Gerda blissfully enjoyed the harmonizing tones of the soldiers. Amid this sensation, Gerda realized that her best chance to get to the river was to wait until the soldiers were the farthest apart from each other, and then make her move.

She waited anxiously for the most opportune time to run. First, she crawled under the barb-wired fence to the restricted guarded area, where she could get a clear space to run at the instant she had the clearest path. Patiently, she waited until the soldiers were marching away. Her anxiety turned to eagerness, as her adrenaline began to surge and the anticipation inside her was building. This was her chance. A few more steps, and she would sprint and swim for her life, literally. When the time came, she got up and ran as fast as she possibly could, just like when she was released from Potsdam. She sprinted without thinking, and kept going until she was able to lunge into a shallow dive like she had practiced all her life for her swim meets. The race was on.

The soldiers noticed the girl running into the river, but were too far away to stop her from plunging into the river. They ran toward her, screaming, partly in disbelief and also in anger. But Gerda was too fast, and timed her break perfectly. Gerda reached the brink of the river and launched. The icy water broke her dive. Gerda was rushing with energy and did not even notice the frigid water. All she was thinking about was swimming as fast as she could. Do not stop until you reach land. She told herself: just keep swimming.

As she crossed the wide border between the East and West, the occasional spotlight would shine around Gerda, tracing her as she raced across the Elbe. She had been training for this her whole life. Always a gifted swimmer, Gerda may have been one of the only girls in Wittenberge capable of taking on such a grueling challenge. Throughout the river, there were small freighter-like buoys or barges, where she would rest periodically. She would hold on only long enough to breathe and continue paddling toward the other side. The rest was short-lived as her will and determination overcame the struggles of her muscles. She kept moving as fast as she could, motivating, pushing, not knowing if she were to be intercepted or caught at any moment by the screaming guards. Her heart was racing like the kind of frightened adrenaline one feels when they are being chased or fear that something is lurking in a dark room. She never looked back.

After what felt like hours, she saw it: the other side. Land was close in her sights, and she kept on paddling through the middle of the night. In pitch dark, with her arms like flabby gelatin, Gerda was about to reach the shore of her freedom. It was the farfetched destination where her freedom was finally attainable. This was the moment she had longed for. She was about to escape from Soviet control to a place where the pressures of communism did not exist. In a few more yards, she would reach a place where she could start fresh and begin a deserved life away from torture and pain. In these last strokes, she was able to be reborn.

Gerda stumbled onto the shore of the other side of the Elbe River and looked back at Wittenberge. Her birthplace was now transformed into a Soviet zone and memory of a lifetime of war and destruction. She had escaped from the years of arrests, prisons, interrogations, and the deaths of friends and family. She was finally in the British occupation zone. Again, she felt relief. This time, the feeling would last longer. Although the memories of trauma, devastation and death would never fully escape her, the tender beginning of a chance to make new memories was gratifying.

In this moment, she thought about her family, too. She felt a love for her parents, who had done nothing but sacrifice their own lives for the safety of their daughter. They covered for her while she hid in the attic, spent all their money to give her an attempt to escape, and held her hand as they looked up at the planes dropping bombs from above. They were always there. She thought about her sister Hannelore, who stayed behind with her own agenda. They may not have had the strong codependent relationship that some siblings forge, but their bond was undeniable and lasting, no matter how hidden or subtle it seemed. Gerda continued to gather her strength as the British troops approached her, rattling in English. Gerda had never deemed it important to learn English in school, but was so pleased to hear it spoken to her. It was the first tangible sign of her escape from East Germany confirming her station in a free zone. The British officer looked at the cold, soaked girl and took her passport. After Germany was divided into four zones, passports were issued for each respective section for travel in between the sectors. With one stamp, the officer returned the document to Gerda where it read, "Illegal Entry".

There was no way that Gerda was going to return to East Germany. She was prepared for death if she had to go back and would not allow the British to make her return. The man looked down at her with apparent pity. It must have been clear just how desperate Gerda really was, shivering, muttering in German. After some deliberation and the first bit of compassion she had seen in years, Gerda was permitted to stay. She did not have to go back to the dismal life that had been instituted for her in East Germany. In the arc of her life, there was so much that she had conquered, endured, and persevered. For Gerda, with the little money she had, and the wet clothes on her back, a journey was about to begin. Even though she accomplished the feat of traversing the Elbe River into West Germany, she had to continue traveling west, until she was able to cross that larger body of water to America. She would need more than the skills of a good swimmer to make that trip. After all of the experiences of her short life on Earth, she was ready to keep going.

Chapter Seven

LIFE AS A REFUGEE (1949-1951)

Gerda was embarking on a fresh start to a new adventure. She had just escaped out of East Germany across the Elbe river into the British occupied zone with only the little bit of money she had. Her family was back in Wittenberge, who also had to continue a new chapter in their life, anxious of what could happen to their daughter. They set one of their children free in hopes she would find a better life. There is always the worry that something could happen that was out of their control. But for Otto and Minna, granting Gerda the possibility of a free and plentiful life was worth the risk. Hannelore had an ulterior motive in staying behind, something that was unknown to Gerda and others until years after. Gerda was arrested on numerous occasions for suspicion of espionage and colluding with plots against the SED and Soviets while her very own sister became a policewoman for the very same organization in Wittenberge. Gerda always thought that the Russians were stupid and their false accusations reflected this notion – especially since Hannelore was the spy all along.

Before Gerda's escape, Hannelore was approached by a representative of the Western front in Germany to work as a spy. Always going a different direction from Gerda, Hannelore accepted the dangerous responsibility, even after seeing the potential repercussions for her sister and many others in Wittenberge. Hannelore took the risk of being a spy and intensified this risk by joining the SED. She played an elemental part in attaining information for the British and Americans in the West. So although Gerda was escaping to pursue her dream, Hannelore was, in a way, helping in that freedom by being a part of the solution, not just idly sitting by as a problem continued.

Gerda knew she had to get as far away from the Elbe River as possible. Just over those choppy waters where she swam to freedom were the Soviet troops. Although she was seemingly safe, her journey to America was just beginning. The farther she was from the East, the closer she felt to making it one day to America. Gerda got onto a bus and continued her escape. It did not matter where she went, as long as she kept moving. She was in a similar state of mind when she was released from Potsdam, frantically running without direction, and elated to be free. Gerda went as far as her money would allow her, paying the minimal fare at the beginning of each stop. Eventually, she ran out of money and was left in the small village of Labenz, truly alone in a place unknown to her. She was now a refugee, someone who had escaped her home to find something better and gratefully given the mere chance to live without duress.

The path to America that Gerda envisioned as a child was starting to take shape. There were two essential steps that Gerda needed to complete in order to realize this dream. She learned that she needed to obtain the proper documentation to travel to the United States, which included an updated passport and sponsorship from a host in America. Upon her escape, the only passport that Gerda possessed was an East German passport, which would not be accepted going from West Germany to the United States. Instead, she needed a West German passport. In order to acquire this document, she had to go to the German consulate in Hamburg to apply, which required money not only to get to the city, but also to pay the application fees. With no money to her name, working hard was the only option. For Gerda, this was not seen as a challenge, but a necessity to continue on with her life. Sponsorship would also be required. Gerda had relatives living in America, who would be willing to sponsor her, that escaped the war years before it escalated to the level that Gerda and her family experienced. The pieces were in place, but it was up to Gerda to put it all together, with the same determination she had to leave East Germany. This feeling was doing nothing but getting stronger as she had to keep her motivation steady.

This small village was in the middle of the country, and was characterized by farmland and an eerie quiet. Other than her short stint as a teacher, Gerda had lived in a city all her life. She was never surrounded by so much space. Exiting the bus to an unfamiliar city with absolutely nowhere to call home or go for safety, Gerda's place in life was of mystery. Gerda had to find some sort of work or place to stay. She knew that in the West, she would not be subject to arrest or oppression. She went from door to door to different farms in the village, seeking an opportunity to do anything that would pay. Eventually, she arrived at Hermann Farm, where the family took her in to work in exchange for a bed to sleep in, food to eat as well as a small wage.

Hermann Farm would be her home for the time being. She shared her room with another East German refugee named Grudel. Sitting in this room on the quaint Hermann Farm in the safe zone of Germany, Gerda for the first time since she could remember felt almost completely at ease. There was no one who was going to come to take her in the middle of the night and no chance of bombs dropping. She only faced the long hours of a working farm day. Although she did not have much experience in this style of work, it was a hardship that she was more than capable of handling, no matter how demanding the workload.

Gerda at Hermann Farm, 1949.

LIFE AS A REFUGEE (1949-1951)

Switching to an agrarian lifestyle was an adjustment for Gerda in comparison to her upbringing in a city during wartime. Gerda was required to be up at five in the morning and continue working until nighttime everyday. The common saying goes that a normal job goes from nine to five. But a farmer's job is from five to nine. Although the physical labor needed to work on a farm may have been arduous for Gerda, in relation to the intensity and true hardships faced in her previous experience made the work all the more tolerable. One of the more tolling tasks that Gerda had to do was to milk cows. She never performed the task before and did not anticipate how difficult it would be. For a girl, it was tough work and required much endurance, especially as the heifer's tail would constantly be whipping her in the face. She was required to milk ten cows in the morning, five at noon, and five at night. At the end of the day, Gerda's hands would ache from the work. Each night, she would hold them up and down in cold and hot water, soothing the pain as best she could. Although painful and challenging, Gerda knew that if she complained about the work or did not do a good job, she would face a more grueling reality. To jeopardize her job at Hermann Farm could have led to losing it, which meant no money, no passport, no home and no trip to America.

Gerda had other duties during her time at Hermann Farm, like planting sugar beets up and down the hills. Planting the sugar beets up the hill was not so bad. Getting proper footing down the hill was difficult, which often led to her falling flat on her face into the dirt. But like all jobs on the farm, they had to get done or else there would be no gratification or reward. Gerda worked through the pain and did anything that was asked by the Hermanns who were quite kind to her for letting Gerda stay at their home and providing her a place to work. Even though the pay was extremely low, it helped her sustain herself. Within the family's accommodation and her situation as a refugee, Gerda could not find another feeling besides appreciation and gratitude toward the Hermanns.

Battling the pain and frustration, Gerda would grind her teeth and keep working. Faith escaped her years earlier, but Gerda began to outlet her emotions in a different way at this juncture of her life. She began to cry regularly. At twenty-one, Gerda endured so much mental anguish in her life that the physical pain she was feeling now in a way symbolized the torment she endured for years before coming to Hermann Farm. Gerda would cry almost daily, uncontrollably sobbing, for a myriad of

The Hermann Family

reasons. From the soreness in her hands to the deep burning desire to get out of Europe to America - her spirit was drained. She just wanted that passport so badly, to get her that much closer to America. Some nights Gerda would stay awake at night, turning in bed thinking of what life would be like when she made it to America. She would also think back to her family in Wittenberge, if they were safe or happy. It was a dueling introspection, weighing the happiness she could attain against the willingness of her family to set her off and stay in the very place she rued being a part of.

Gerda had been in contact with her aunt and uncle, who escaped from Europe, about getting a sponsorship to allow her to go to the United States. They agreed and Gerda was set to fill all the requirements to make her final pilgrimage to America. Before her year was finished working at the farm, Gerda finally had enough money. She took the train to Hamburg and applied for a West German passport. With her aunt and uncle agreeing to sponsor her, Gerda now simply had to bide her time and hope that all the paperwork would be approved to enable her to travel across the pond to America.

At times, the Hermanns would send Gerda by bicycle to run small errands for them. Usually she would go to the market, the post office or pharmacist to get a few things for herself and the family. In doing so, she met many people. She continued to work hard in an attempt to earn money to be able to go to Hamburg and get her passport. Although she was grateful for the Hermann's hospitality, over an entire year she only saved enough money to buy one pair of black shoes and pay for her passport in Hamburg. On one of her trips to the pharmacy, she was given an opportunity to work with one of the pharmacists as a maid for their family. After a year of working with cows and sugar beets and all other rigorous duties, Gerda seized the opportunity, which not only promised better conditions, but also paid more.

Gerda spent the following year working for the pharmacist as the family maid in the village of Steinhorst. Her duties were as expected for a housekeeper including cleaning, cooking, and managing most of the household duties. It was a refreshing change of pace, in a way, to be part of a home, cooking something other than boiled potato sandwiches and bread with butter like she used to in East Germany. Although she was not a professional like her employer, for Gerda this was a major step up from shoveling animal waste and milking cows. All the while, Gerda continued to dream of her future life in America, saving every penny she could to attain the means to get there. She would still wonder about her family's well being from time to time, but her focus was squarely in the other direction.

Pharmacists and doctors have reciprocal relationships, so they interacted regularly in those days. One of the doctors that Gerda worked with, as part of her duties with the pharmacist, offered her a job as an assistant. Gerda accepted and already felt the hard work and emotional toll of escaping East Germany paying off. This was the most elite position that Gerda had ever held in her life. Such a job would be almost impossible to attain in East Germany after the war, only two years removed from escape. Since her arrival with absolutely nothing, soaked and alone in a new life, she had reached relative success in contrast to being brutalized and malnourished just a few short years ago in East Germany.

It was during this time that Gerda started to embrace life more, rather than simply trying to coast by without confrontation. She set goals, felt comfortable in her position in life, and had a clear plan for starting anew in America. In the past two years before being hired by the doctor, Gerda had bit her lip, put her head down and worked as hard as she could to continue her life as a free girl, hoping one day to make it to America. This was her top priority. Socializing and recreational activities were not worth the risk of compromising a job that she considered herself fortunate to have. After some time settling into her position at the doctor's office, Gerda started to go to dances and socials in town. There, she would for the first time in nearly ten years let her hair loose, meet new people, and dance like she did as a girl. Gerda was always an excellent dancer and did not have problem getting along with people at the socials. But it was not all fun. Many people from West Germany were not receptive to the refugees from East Germany, accusing East Germans of taking their jobs. Before one dance Gerda attended, she entered a ping-pong tournament. She did not know that it was there that she would meet somebody who would change her life in a way that she had not been directed before, one of love and happiness.

Chapter Eight

LONGING FOR AMERICA AND LOVE
(1951-1952)

Gerda entered a ping-pong tournament one night and was randomly matched against a boy named Karl Senner, a fit guy from East Prussia with a large smile. The two played against each other. Afterwards, they eyed each other from across the room, reluctant to talk to each other before everyone headed to a dance. At the social, Karl finally approached Gerda and asked her to dance with him. Gerda, flattered, accepted and accompanied Karl on the dance floor, where they stayed for quite a while. Gerda was immediately impressed by the handsome man and his dancing skills, which were almost as good as hers. The two of them had fun for hours and continued to see each other afterwards. Gerda was first attracted to Karl through dance but by way of his courtship, began to learn more about the young man that she even then knew would one day be her loving husband.

Karl was from a small village called Kunegsblat in what was then Prussia, a former empire east of Germany that no longer exists. Karl grew up as an only child, and dealt through much tragedy. His parents had attempted to have other children a few times but the child miscarried or died as an infant in each case. This was extremely traumatic for his mother Helene, who was not mentally stable during his childhood. Whether this emotional instability was attributable to these deaths or something else, Karl's father, who was also named Karl, had to endure his wife's erratic behavior for longer than he could bear. Karl and Helene exhibited an unhealthy marriage. In turn, their son Karl had a rough upbringing, living with parents that had their own clear problems with each other and, like Gerda, living in a time of war and the dissipation of his country.

Besides being three years older, Gerda had much in common with Karl. His father worked for the railroad company before being enlisted in the war. Karl was also a member of the Hitler Youth. He, too, was a refugee, who escaped with his mother from the East after the war ended. The Russians also occupied his town and the Soviet troops proved to be too dangerous. Like Wittenberge, their town was an unfit place for them to live, forcing his mother to escape with her son. His father, however, was not as loving as Gerda's. With Helene continuing to unravel, Karl's father abandoned his family after the war. Karl's father left for the war, never to return, not from death or battle, but for his own selfish reasons. He found a new wife, and started another family. Karl understood why his father left his mother, but it was a bit unsettling to be left without a father in a time of deep turmoil and chaos as well as through adolescence, through no fault of his own.

Karl and Gerda, from then on, spent most of their free time together, taking long walks and confiding in each other not just about their pasts and their current lives as refugees, but also the future. Karl had a bicycle and Gerda would hop on the handlebars as they coasted together on windy roads. Gerda had not had her own bicycle since the Soviets took it from her, or the few times that her employers allowed her to go on errands. Karl and Gerda also always enjoyed dancing together. Like the first social after the ping-pong tournament, they would always go to different dances where and when they could, winning a number of trophies in the process. As long as there was water, Gerda loved to swim and, as long as they had each other, Gerda knew she could love and dance. They were excellent dancers and even better companions. Over time, their love grew stronger and stronger and their relationship more intimate. They would talk over their ambitions and Gerda continued to speak of America and how she was destined to make it there, while Karl was content with his place in West Germany. He was satisfied to be away from the chaos and drama that had followed him most of his life. West Germany provided a feeling of complacency for refugees, offering a livelihood essentially free from harm, but Gerda dreamed of more.

As 1951 was coming to an end, Gerda was set to go to America in a few months. She finally had her papers processed, her passport intact, and her aunt and uncle in America were providing her a boat ticket to travel over. This was an unexpected turn of events for Gerda, who in a way found a new reason for life in the love and companionship from Karl. This left Gerda with a new personal struggle: love or life? Her family risked so much to get her to this point, and she endured much trauma to be in a position to finally realize her dream in getting to America. Yet here, in her new home of West Germany, she found love. She could go on forever dancing and taking long strolls in an idyllic romance, or set across the Atlantic Ocean to whatever new opportunities loomed in America, as she always intended.

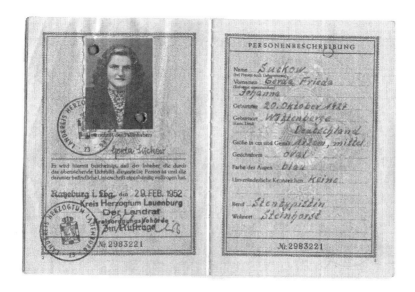

One night, when the doctor and his wife left for Hamburg, Gerda snuck into their room to borrow the wife's dress for a dance with Karl. The long, beautiful dress was unlike anything Gerda had ever worn or imagined she could afford, cascading to the floor. Gerda's intention was just to borrow the dress for the night. She wanted to look nice for Karl and feel good about herself, before returning it without getting caught. Karl was very impressed with how she looked in the dress, in awe of how it illuminated her beauty. All her friends and others approached her at the dance admiring how lovely and elegant she looked. After an exhilarating night, Gerda returned home to have the doctor and his wife waiting for her earlier than expected.

LONGING FOR AMERICA AND LOVE (1951-1952)

The repercussions were messy as the employers were nothing short of displeased and furious with Gerda for betraying their trust. Although she intended to return it, the doctor and his wife accused Gerda of stealing the dress from their closet. The doctor and his wife contemplated how to deal with the matter. Gerda grew anxious as they considered whether to reprimand, fire her, or perhaps worse. By pressing charges against Gerda, she could have faced arrest, and there were a number of fateful results that could have compromised her trip to America or her life away from East Germany. Gerda began to get very worried. What if she could not go to America? What if she was arrested? Could she handle another stint in prison? Would they send her back to East Germany? A simple lapse in judgment that led to a harmless night with a new dress could cost her everything, she thought.

The doctor and his wife decided not to press charges or have Gerda arrested, but they did fire her. Disappointed yet relieved, Gerda had only weeks to spare before her ship was set to leave for America. The only significantly poor decision she had ever made in her life almost unraveled all her progress toward getting to America. Suddenly, she realized the danger of staying in Germany. It would be foolish to potentially have something similar happen again by staying here for anyone, even if it was the man she loved. Karl pleaded with her to stay, be with him, and live their lives together. But Gerda refused. She risked and sacrificed too much to abandon her plan now. She left her family behind and endured many trying events and the payoff had finally arrived. Gerda told Karl to come to America.

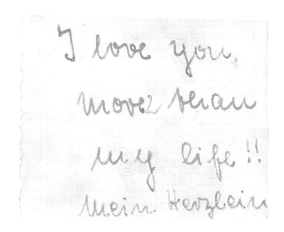

Karl did not have any relatives in America, or anywhere else besides his mentally ill mother. His father abandoned him, and his siblings never lived to even walk. The only life that he knew was right in front of him. He did not want this purity of love to escape him. In West Germany, he and Gerda were free, had a pleasant social life and more importantly, each other. However, the unknown allure of America had always attracted Gerda since she was a child and she risked too much to realize this dream. She decided that there was no way that she could stay and that if Karl wanted to, then he would have to live in Germany without her. Gerda promised she would get him a sponsor. No matter how difficult it would be, no matter how long it would take, she would make the necessary strides so that they could be together. Together, she vowed that one day they would both start a new life in America. Gerda had to leave until then.

Chapter Nine

LIFE ACROSS THE POND (1952-1955)

The day had finally arrived. Gerda had her ticket in her hand to travel across the Atlantic Ocean by boat to America. Everything was sorted and her ticket purchased for the SS America by her aunt and uncle. Karl promised to write Gerda every day that they were apart. By the same token, Gerda assured him that she would get a sponsor for him so they could be together in America. Gerda walked to the dock with what belongings she had and boarded the ship. She was finally stepping out of Europe to yet another new locale, making her permanent escape from Germany.

The S.S. America

The ticket was reserved for business class, a status that she never attained on her own and did not know of. Her aunt and uncle were wealthy, respected people and had the resources to provide this for her. Gerda did not fit into this class, though. She certainly did not have the clothes for it nor had much in common with the other rich people lodging in the section. The vessel she was on was enormous, like a giant building turned on its side. Each level of the ship she was on represented a different social class, with the wealthiest passengers staying at the top. When first boarding the vessel, Gerda felt uneasy. She was happy to be heading to America, but had a hard time picturing what life would be like once she arrived. She knew she wanted to go there, even as a child, but she did not know why. There were the usual concerns like not knowing the language or the people, but the driving force in Gerda's spirit was telling her that this was her goal to live free, start fresh, and make a new life. To Gerda, it was the land of milk and honey, but it also seemed like a fantasy. Gerda was not as much anxious as she was eager to see what her reality would amount to in America, from the physical landscape of the country to the variety of people she would invariably meet, and the overall life that she would develop for herself in this modern world.

Gerda on board the S.S. America on her way to New York, 1952

Gerda left Europe for America in March of 1952. It took ten days to get to America. She was accommodated in business class with the rich, but felt more comfortable with other refugees and people of her status in the lower deck. She would sneak down when she could. There, she and the others would sing, dance, and of course drink. They were all eager to be leaving Europe and heading to the opportunity that lay ahead in America. People of many different nationalities and accumulated histories were traveling to America with their own agendas and ideas of prosperity. With the other refugees, she shared stories and ambitions as well as laughter, something that had become an infrequent activity for Gerda in her short life. There were a variety of troubling tales and experiences throughout the war and whatever else had led them to be on the very same boat. For all the comfort they provided, these moments were short-lived, as Gerda spent most of her time in her designated cabin in business class. There, everyone was dressed to kill and she had nothing to wear. She felt strange and isolated, often sitting in her cabin thinking of her place in the world, let alone the ship. She did not think she belonged here nor there, feeling truly displaced - she thought she belonged overboard. Anxiety continued to build as the days went on and the ship moved closer to shore. She had not seen her aunt and uncle for nearly her entire life, as they had left Europe well before the war had seen its most troubling days.

When Gerda arrived to America, she could not understand anything. From the people's language to the commotion of people rushing to their families or being guided to their next destination, she was lost in the chaos. There was nobody waiting for Gerda when the SS America arrived in New York City. Her aunt and uncle lived in Chicago, so she had to get to the train station. She was finally in America, but was not swept with a feeling of prosperity and relief as she imagined when she was a girl. Things seemed hectic and bleak at first. The walk over to the train station was scary for her, as she had to walk through bad parts of town, with people barking things at her in foreign languages. This was when she first realized that adapting to a new place with completely different appearances and customs would be difficult. Even people's appearances were different than she was used to in Germany. She was initially scared of the first black person she saw in New York. This reaffirmed that she was in a totally new place and would encounter many new experiences. Her time may have been easier had she taken English classes more seriously as a child. People doubted she would make it here, but as Gerda boarded the train and settled into her seat, she sighed with at least some comfort. As the train began to leave New York, she realized that her journey never seemed to stop. Whether she was actually traveling or going through her own personal evolutions, Gerda was always required to adapt and change to her surroundings.

Gerda traversed across the Midwest by train to Chicago. She imagined that she was about to see the land of milk and honey, basking in the sunshine of freedom and opportunity that is America. But as the train began to cruise across the heartland to Chicago, Gerda did not see the paradise she expected. Whether all train stations were set in bad parts of town, or Gerda's expectations of the landscape of America was an unrealistic utopia, she could not help but feel that there was nothing but poor and dangerous neighborhoods in this new country. She looked out her window to see shabby towns and dim settings. A peculiar pattern did emerge, however. Gerda noticed that there were two types of buildings that were picturesque in contrast to everything else outside her window.

Among the gritty homes, the veterinarian's offices and funeral parlors were beautiful to Gerda, having Victorian architecture and a comforting and welcoming motif. It was puzzling to Gerda that the most glamorous places looked to be where people and pets go to die, but the strangeness to her trip across America only reflected her uneasiness about the new life that was about to begin in Chicago, where her aunt and uncle were waiting for her.

Her aunt and uncle had a very interesting life as well, including their escape from Germany. It was not as dangerous as Gerda's, but noteworthy nonetheless. Anna, Gerda's aunt, was Otto's sister. She married Marek Weber, a famous German violinist and a full-blooded Jew. They came over to live in America as early as 1936. Although related by blood, Gerda acquired a strong distaste for Anna while she admired Marek, not solely because of his professional achievements as a world-renowned musician, but because he was a loving and compassionate man who tended for his unknown niece.

Anna and Marek Weber, 1948

Anna met Marek by being employed as his secretary. He was originally married to a different woman, but through years of working closely and her own selfish cunning, Anna drew him away from his marriage, and he left his wife. Marek was an extremely famous violinist, known not just in Germany and Europe, but also around the world. Born in Budapest, Marek had his own orchestra by the time his was ten years old. With his innate talents, he went on to lead a number of famed orchestras, as well as write many memorable compositions in what was then modern or parlor jazz. With masterful dexterity, Marek was a virtuoso at his craft. He gained recognition for his records and compositions, and collaborated with pillars of music like Arturo Toscanini, who Gerda later met because of her uncle. Another large part of Marek's life was his religion, Judaism, which ultimately led Anna and him away from their home country of Germany to the United States.

Back in the beginning phases of Hitler's rise to Chancellor and leading the Third Reich, Marek and Anna were living in Berlin, where Marek was actively working and performing as both a violinist and a conductor. Around this time, Hitler ordered the exile of all Jews in Germany. Heeding the warning, Weber cautiously prepared for what could have been the wisest decision he made in his life. He left Germany with Anna for Switzerland, where they lived in Zurich outside Hitler's reach. Gerda's father once visited the couple in Zurich, and was arrested for convening with a Jew upon his return. Marek took this as an indication of the looming persecution that was inevitably to come and decided that it would be in his best interest to leave Europe for America, where he would fully be out of the Nazi's influence. Due to Marek's professional and famed stature, he had viable connections and it was not too difficult for him to relocate to America. In 1936, the Webers settled in Chicago. There, they circumvented the hardships of World War II and established themselves as pillars of the community due to Marek's accolades and accomplishments as a violinist.

Marek Weber with his violin.

Then there was Gerda, someone they had not seen for almost the entirety of her life. They were ignorant to nearly every traumatic experience she endured over the last twenty years. To Gerda, Anna was a manipulative woman, who had her husband wrapped around her finger. Marek, on the other hand, was a kind-hearted man who did not have a hurtful bone in his body. His fingers were so tender from playing the violin that he could not even touch a blade of grass, which mirrored his soft and submissive personality. The opposite of Marek, Anna would at times fake heart attacks to have Marek swoon over her. Gerda was able to assess her manipulative methods and resented her for it. In the short period of time they met, Gerda could easily see that Anna's intentions were not completely sincere. Marek would try to provide for Gerda in any way he could. Anna, however, did not have the same sentiment, undermining Marek from the beginning in secret and making Gerda's transition to America more arduous.

When Gerda got off the train in Chicago to meet her aunt and uncle, Anna quickly began to mistreat Gerda. She scolded the young woman for not being able to speak English. Anna was concerned that being associated with a poor refugee who did not even speak the language would embarrass the status couple. This welcoming frustrated Gerda. After all, Anna herself barely spoke a lick of English even though she had been living a cushy life in America for more than fifteen years while Gerda evaded death. Gerda soon realized that every action Anna made was calculated to avoid her own humiliation. The first example was the boat ticket they purchased for her. Gerda now understood that the expensive business class fare was not out of love or sympathy, but so that Anna would not feel embarrassed about having a poor person come over in the bottom of the ship. Despite the recent findings about Anna's motives, this was Gerda's newest station in life, and she was grateful to be taken in by her family and eager to begin her idealized life in America. After the salutations were exchanged, the trio set off to Marek and Anna's farm in Whitewater, Wisconsin, where they lived during the warmer seasons.

Marek-Anna Farm in Whitewater, WI

The Webers cleverly named the farm Marek-Anna farm. Approaching the farm for the first time, Gerda marveled at the long white picket fence, just like Heidi saw in the books she read as a girl. There was a small cottage next to the large house where Anna and Marek stayed, which Gerda would call her new home. Gerda walked into the cottage and finally felt the rush of emotion that she had been searching for in her escape from East Germany. After many years, she found the warmth of a *real* home filled with security and ease. There was one full-sized bed along with everything needed for her to happily stay during her time on the farm. Gerda looked at the bed and thought about Karl, and how this would be a perfect place for the both of them. Gerda felt alone in the room. She could not help thinking about the absence of the loved one in her life, more determined than ever to bring him to America. Together, they would live a loving life in this new land, but for now, she had to bide her time without him. She took a picture of the bed and sent it to him saying "Doesn't it look like it's fit for 2?"

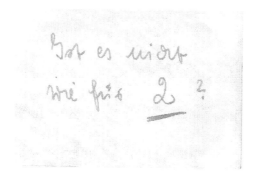

Gerda's bedroom in Whitewater, WI.

LIFE ACROSS THE POND (1952-1955)

At this gentleman's farm, which was more of a getaway than a cultivation plot, they had some dairy and other minor chores that needed standard maintenance. Gerda, along with one other gentleman who had always worked at the farm, was set to work right away to help maintain the estate. She pulled weeds and painted the very fence that made her feel so welcomed. She was paid only five dollars a week but was once again grateful to be taken in, this time, in such a safe and pleasant space. Gerda quickly learned that the generosity from the Webers was not as seemingly unconditional as family would expect.

Marek was quite affable given his career and social position, and had no problem with purchasing the business class ticket that enabled Gerda to get to New York and then to Chicago. But Anna had a different motive. She was tabulating a bill for Gerda, from the first instance that she applied for sponsorship in Hamburg. Initially, unbeknownst to Marek, Anna intended to make Gerda pay her back for every cent that they had spent on her behalf. This ultimately meant that everything that Gerda would work for on the farm would essentially go back to Anna to pay for the business class boat trip, the train ticket to Chicago and all other expenses doled out by the couple.

Gerda still had her sole pair of black shoes that she had bought with her year's earnings working as a refugee in Germany. She held this material possession close to her. Not only was it one of the nicer things she owned, but it represented a life beyond rations to Gerda. As a child, she was never granted a pair of shoes that were bought exclusively for her. She was only provided misfit shoes by the government through rationing. The pair of black shoes she bought was also a symbol of an entire year's work on Hermann farm, where she came with nothing and strenuously and laboriously *earned* those shoes. This was a sentimental item for Gerda that she held preciously, to remind her of what it truly takes to make something for herself. For now, she just kept working, waiting until Karl could eventually come to America and they could start their lives together as planned. Gerda told the Webers about her love and they agreed to sponsor him. Although this action was greatly appreciated, it was not sincere from Anna, who would constantly extort Gerda and taunt her, saying that she would drop the sponsorship if she did not do what she said, act like she wanted, or pay for everything that was granted to her.

 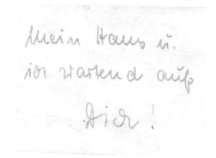

Gerda at her cottage in Whitewater, WI. "My house, and I'm waiting for you!"

While working at the Wisconsin farm over the course of the next few months, a few things happened that counteracted the vindictive relationship that Anna held over Gerda. Firstly, as Karl promised, he wrote Gerda a letter every single day on airmail paper. These were not postcards or brief sentiments, but rather full hand-written letters, front and back, professing his love and devotion to Gerda. In turn, Gerda wrote back when she could, often sending small pictures with meaningful phrases on the back about how her paradise was almost complete and he was the only thing missing.

Marek-Anna Farm in Whitewater, Wisconsin

87

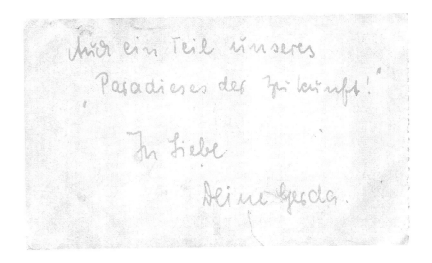

"This, too, is a part of our paradise of the future. Love, Your Gerda."

Another happiness for Gerda was her relationship with Marek, who she grew to love and respect so much that she confided in him about her experiences through the war, Potsdam, and her escape. Marek, a sensitive, loving man, solaced Gerda and tried to appease her every wish without asking for anything in return. He would buy her gifts like dresses and leather handbags, beautiful items that Gerda never imagined herself owning. However, Anna would take note of these gifts and put them on the ever-growing bill for Gerda that she was required to pay back in exchange for the couple's sponsorship and support.

As the summer came to an end, they all headed back to Chicago, where Anna and Marek lived in a beautiful apartment on Lakeshore Drive, right beside the beauty that is Lake Michigan, which is still a prime location today. There was no room for Gerda to stay there, according to Anna, so they brought her to the McCormick YWCA. Gerda was to stay there while they were in Chicago. Like most interactions with Gerda, Anna had ulterior motives. It was here that Anna ordered Gerda learn to speak English, as to not further humiliate her.

Gerda walked into the YWCA and was approached by an employee. The woman registered Gerda and warmly welcomed her with a bed to stay in. After a struggle in communication, where she realized Gerda was German, the woman asked Gerda to follow her. Gerda followed the woman who had been nothing but receptive, wondering where she was being led to. The woman then pointed to a group of other girls and motioned her toward their direction with a smile as she left the room. Gerda approached the girls and said hello. As she greeted them, she quickly realized that the small group of four girls that she was about to meet were German as well.

Gerda outside the McCormick YWCA in Chicago, IL.

Anna forced Gerda into the YWCA to learn English and be submerged in the language and culture. Ironically, the exact opposite played out, as Gerda quickly became best friends with the German girls. They all identified with each other as refugees. She was thrilled. Gerda finally felt a sense of camaraderie that she had lacked since her days in the Hitler Youth. Gerda took the time in YWCA to learn English and truly assimilate to American life. With worthy friends and budding exposure to the United States' way of living, her life in America was beginning to develop and bloom. All the time, Karl continued to write Gerda each and every day. Gerda saved every letter, some nights leafing through the dozens of papers, reminiscing on memories past and thinking about their future together.

Chapter Ten

LIFE WITH KARL (1953-1955)

About a year had passed since Gerda arrived to America. In that time, all the paperwork was sorted for Karl's arrival. Gerda was itching with anticipation, as this was the moment she had been looking forward to since she first arrived to New York. She longed to be reunited with the love of her life in the country she dreamed about as a little girl. Everything was set in place, and she eagerly waited for Karl to arrive to Chicago. She collected the hundreds of airmail letters she had organized into a neat little notebook, representing their love. Soon, the collection would become a relic. There would no longer be a need for more letters. Gerda had imagined this since she had arrived to Chicago, a picturesque realization of the American dream, free from occupation or inherent harm, with her partner in love and life by her side.

Karl arrived and they held each other in their arms, embracing to express their prolonged love. Karl never imagined he would make it to America. As a young refugee without a father, the only future he had grown to expect was the simpleton's life he made for himself in West Germany. Here in America, he was now with the girl he loved in a big city in a new country, with no knowledge of the language or insight to where life would lead the couple next. Karl was less adventurous than Gerda in their paths to America, but together they stood, no longer running or escaping. Reunited at last, they could simply live, and flourish.

Karl began his assimilation to America in a similar manner as Gerda, staying in the YMCA as he settled in and figured out where he was to begin working. He arranged to work on a farm in Hebron, Illinois, while

LIFE WITH KARL (1953-1955)

Gerda continued with her duties on the Marek-Anna farm in Whitewater, Wisconsin. Anna and Marek were receptive to Karl. After all, their sponsorship enabled him to come and stay in America. If anything, this was no benefit to them at all, but instead to Gerda. Although Anna gave Gerda a hard time through their lives together in Chicago, Gerda was the only real family that Anna had in America. This was her brother's daughter. Somewhere below her cruel and malevolent personality, there surely laid some sympathy for Gerda.

Yet, the only apparent interactions that Anna had with Gerda were manipulative. She constantly threatened to drop Karl's sponsorship, or billed Gerda with every gift that her husband bought for her. Soon after Karl's arrival, Marek bought Gerda a car. Gerda, had barely ever even ridden in a car, and was completely floored by the gesture. It brought her to tears, not of joy, but of desperation. She graciously sobbed to Marek, but asked him nicely to stop buying her presents because she could not afford it. Marek was confused. Gerda then explained to him how she had been paying off debts to Anna, dating all the way back from the ticket to America. Marek was embarrassed. Though he did not fully approve of his wife's actions, he was not completely surprised. He was somewhat aware of the deviousness his wife was capable of, but was blinded by his own love from fully seeing her ways. She would consistently fake heart attacks and faint in order to draw attention. Gerda hated the fact that this generous, compassionate man spent so much time on his knees catering to Anna in an unneeded manner.

When she returned to the farm in Whitewater, Gerda wanted nothing more than to start her life with Karl. Still aided by the sponsorship from Anna and Marek, they did not have the means or funds to care for themselves so they were in no position to be completely independent just yet. Anna provided a home for them, and then offered it to be their permanent residence. Gerda was thrilled to learn that the farm with the picket white fence could be theirs. She dreamed of sharing the bed with Karl that she once saw as a slice of paradise for them. However, in true Anna fashion, there was a condition to living in the farmhouse: they were not to have children. For Gerda, this unreasonable request was the last straw. She was fed up with placating Anna and compromising her life with Karl in exchange. Gerda decided that she would no longer put up with her demands and left Whitewater in the middle of the night. She went back to Chicago to meet Karl and begin their life independently, no matter how difficult and trying it may be.

Gerda returned to the YWCA and Karl to the YMCA, where they started looking for jobs on their own. Even though they were starting from nothing, anything attained from here on out would be theirs alone, and that was something that would make them both content. Anna, who was always concerned about how she and her husband appeared within their circles of friends, was embarrassed and humiliated by Gerda's sudden departure. Anna and Marek called Gerda, pleading not to leave them and to consider staying. The couple reminded Gerda that they had no heir to their large estate. If she were to stay with them, then eventually the farm would all be theirs one day, Anna and Marek said. But for Gerda, even the promise of securing wealth was not worth compromising the life and family that she and Karl would build. Gerda told them to take their money and throw it in Lake Michigan. If living according to Anna and Marek's demands was the means to attaining their fortune, she was not interested. Gerda had already come so far on her own, enduring struggles, that she was not willing to complacently live an unfulfilling life in exchange for some financial security. She had fled to freedom away from oppression and would not be limited by someone who did not have an authoritative role in her life as in Germany. Ironically, even though Anna and Marek did not have any pets or children, they ended up donating their entire estate to animal shelters and orphanages instead of Gerda and Karl.

Like many of the immigrants and refugees who also retreated to Chicago, Gerda and Karl had to begin their lives modestly, obtaining whatever work they could, without the networks, finances, or education that other Americans had to help them start up. Karl began to work as a mechanic for a Swedish man. Gerda got employed at the World Book Encyclopedia as a file clerk, even though she did not have a strong grip on the English language. Other German girls worked at World Book, which is how Gerda heard about the position. With newly-acquired jobs, Karl and Gerda were on their way to being independent and getting their own place to live. The two were working hard and moving forward in their lives, but their relationship was still going through some growing pains.

Gerda began to feel some distance from Karl. For some reason, things were not as picturesque as she had envisioned. At that point, Gerda had been living in the United States by herself for more than a year, while Karl had been going about his simple life in West Germany.

LIFE WITH KARL (1953-1955)

Gerda had an extra year to adjust to this new way of living and Karl was just not at the same level as Gerda when it came to learning the English language, the United States culture, and people's attitudes. Little things he did bothered her, and at times he even seemed unreasonable. They were almost codependent for a while, which went against Gerda's desires. Gerda had always foreseen a life for herself in America from when she was a little girl, but only had the aspiration to share this with a loved one when she met Karl. At first, Gerda was concerned that their relationship may muddle the progress she was seeking to attain in assimilating and thriving in America. She then made the difficult decision to break up with Karl. At the time, it seemed like the right thing to do.

Soon after, Karl started to date one of Gerda's friends. At first, Gerda was surprised and then started to reflect on the arc of their relationship. She thought about where they came from, how they got there, and the troubles they endured. Whether it stemmed from jealousy or a sudden epiphany, Gerda was not happy to see Karl in a new relationship and thought to the roots of their romance at the ping-pong tournament years before. It did not take long for Gerda to realize that she loved him, and they were meant to be together. They got back together, worked through their struggles and decided to get married soon after.

The wedding was a small ceremony in January of 1954. More bottles were consumed afterwards than people in attendance. Besides the couple, the only others there were their friends Ingrid and Andy Ludolf. The couple stood before the judge as he presided over the marriage. By this point, Gerda had a decent grasp of the English language and was able to understand a fair amount of what the judge was saying. Even with her strong English skills, she could not comprehend everything that was being said, nor could anyone else in the room. At one point, Gerda and Karl had to repeat a few lines the judge said. Karl's English was very poor, though, and as he tried to recite what the judge was saying, laughter and chuckling from Gerda and their two friends echoed throughout the room. They may as well have been talking nonsense lines and gibberish. Ultimately, they knew that marriage vows do not really change in translation, and it was still the official statement of their love and commitment to each other.

Karl and Gerda's wedding day, 1954

Gerda had a lifelong bout with God and exactly where to place his existence in the context of her life and now of her family's. Gerda lost her faith after carrying loads of burnt dead bodies, one after the other, back in Wittenberge and her disbelief was reaffirmed during her arrest in Potsdam. Karl, however, was a Catholic. Given that their marriage meant compromise as well as sharing their lives, she decided to give Catholicism another try in Chicago for him and their future children. She met with a priest, who asked her how long it was since she lost faith and had been to church. Gerda replied about five or six years. The priest looked down, then at Gerda, and sympathetically told her that she should forget about it, that there was simply no hope for her. This was the final straw to her relationship with the Catholic Church. Every phase of her life where the church had an opportunity to reinsert itself or apply to her life situation, something would always happen to counter it.

Now, with their new family and jobs, they finally were able to move into their own home. In Chicago, there were a number of different neighborhoods inhabited by European immigrants. In one enclave, there were all Russians and in another all Germans and so on. Karl and Gerda first moved into a Polish neighborhood. They had a furnished upstairs apartment with an entrance through the back stairwell. The apartment had a small kitchenette, and a shared bathroom with a woman that they surprisingly never met. The apartment was located above a bar, a common feature of the neighborhood. The streets were constantly littered with beer and liquor bottles, as if they were a part of the pavement itself. The Senners always had to tiptoe or step over and around the broken glass and empty cans each time they entered or exited the place.

As they began to settle into their new lives, now with a new home, new jobs and new friends, Gerda was feeling better and better about the course of their lives since becoming fully independent in America. In their mid-twenties, Gerda and Karl had a fresh, youthful spirit that had at times passed them by, given their history. This meant laughing with friends, getting into exciting situations, and feeling happy just living away from oppression and danger. In the coming months, Gerda got pregnant with her first child as did her four friends she met on her first day at the YWCA. Karl and Gerda realized that with the expected addition to their family, many changes would have to be made.

First, they decided to take English lessons much more seriously. Living in a neighborhood where everyone spoke either Polish or German was certainly an easy adjustment. But they felt they were responsible to provide every opportunity for their child, and that started with giving him the ability to speak the native language. Each day after work they traveled by bus to the YMCA to take English lessons, before returning home to make dinner. They did this five nights a week, relentlessly working then studying. This type of dedication is not seen as abundantly today. For nearly the entire year, they maintained this schedule.

Gerda and friends walking about Lake Michigan in Chicago, IL.

Gerda, who had always been a good student, was able to read and write by the end of the year. She was never satisfied with her progress. Even after she attained those skills, she would still translate phrases in her head, which was bothersome because she knew in order to be fluent, one must think in that language. She would meet people who would ask what country she was from, England or Germany, a question that deeply annoyed her. Gerda wanted to be seen as a woman living in America, not just an immigrant. However, for only a little more than a year of education, her progress was extremely impressive. She was increasingly able to communicate with people in different situations whether it was for work or leisure. Even when resorting to the highest level of education at universities, professors told her that her speech was excellent. Still, Gerda always looked not to just succeed, but excel.

The Senners also realized that they would need to live in a cheaper home, seeing that they would have another mouth to feed. They first went to an Italian neighborhood. Within a few weeks, they decided to leave as the Italian people and its language became too much to bear for the couple. With their fast talking, completely different than the Slavic languages that Karl and Gerda were accustomed to, the two thought it would be better to find a different home, one where they could furnish it themselves and relate better with the people in the neighborhood.

Ultimately, they went back to the North Side of Chicago, on Sawyer Street. They only had a sofa that pulled out to a bed, some end tables, lamps, one chair, a kitchen set with a stove, and a baby buggy. Most of the furniture was very cheap, and upholstered in thick black nylon. Most importantly though, they were able to purchase their own furniture, after years of taking only what they could carry, truly making it *their* home. The apartment sat below the street with small windows looking out just a foot above the sidewalk. Gerda and Karl would sit at night, looking up as they watched people's feet bustling past their home.

At the end of December 1954, before the Senners were going to celebrate New Year's Eve, a surprise came that changed how the year played out. Gerda entered labor with her first child. The couple rushed to St. Joseph's, a Catholic hospital, where Gerda had a doctor who was coincidentally from Germany on internship. Gerda began a laborious birth that lasted nearly twenty-eight hours. The doctor insisted that Gerda would need a cesarean section because the situation was getting critical and the most important objective was to get the baby out alive. When the doctor called for the nuns to help assist with the procedure, Gerda overheard an argument that had hit her to the core, touching on her previous bouts with faith and God.

The nuns refused to assist in the C-section, knowing about Gerda's conflict with God and the Catholic Church. Gerda overheard a phrase uttered by one of the nuns, a type of reasoning that she would never forget. The nun rationalized that they would not assist in the C-section because "she is going out of life, and the baby is coming into life." To Gerda, this indicated that the nurses were indifferent about her dying from this birth. They wanted no more unfaithful children to come from her in the future. With Gerda's death, the child would counteract her life by turning to faith, the nuns believed. Gerda had had problems with that Catholic Church ever since she started seeing the horrors of war. Throughout her life, there were clarifying incidents that reassured and solidified her stance on the Catholic Church. This was one of them. Finally, the doctor urged and insisted that the C-section had to be done, or nobody would live. The caesarean was performed without the help of anesthesia. Gerda gave birth to a baby boy.

Although this experience was yet another painful and arduous event in Gerda's life, she survived. Two days later as Gerda was in recovery with her son, the very same nuns from the birth room came to Gerda's room and sat beside her bed, asking her if she would like to go to the commune where she and the child could be cared for. Gerda, furious at the duplicitous actions of the nuns, withheld her emotions and politely told them no. The nuns respected her wishes, only to return the following day with the same request. Gerda, a bit more agitated this time, ordered them out of her room. On the very next day, the nuns came back, yet again, baring the same message to lure Gerda back to the Catholic Church. By this point, Gerda had no more tolerance for the church or these deceitful women who she saw representing it. She reacted by throwing a telephone across the room directly at the two nuns. She no longer believed in the church and wanted no part in it. The nuns now understood this sentiment quite clearly.

With the birth of Ralph, Gerda and Karl further validated the makeup of their lives in America with a family, a home, and a complete life. All the suffering they endured and places to which they fled were leading to this moment. It was the closest thing for Gerda to the paradise that she envisioned, even as a little girl reading those books. She was living in America, married to the man she loved, with a beautiful healthy baby boy. Just before this joyous occasion, another event was thrown into the mix that would alter their plans yet again, sending the family on a journey across the States, away from the life they built. Karl received a letter from the United States government with some telling and surprising news that could not be avoided. Even though they escaped and evaded war and persecution that they thought was now thousands of miles away and years behind them, Karl was drafted into the United States military.

Chapter Eleven

A FAMILY ON THE MOVE (1955-1957)

When Karl received his draft card, he was confused at first. Not only had he just come from Europe as a refugee of World War II, but his citizenship had also not yet been granted. He was here on sponsorship, and had not yet gone through the appropriate steps to become a permanent citizen. His English was not even passable. Karl thought he left the war behind him. He previously vowed never to go in uniform again, never wanting to see even a bellboy's outfit. But, there was no evading this process as many people were drafted during this time. Karl did not want to compromise the livelihood of his new family and the life they created in Chicago. He headed down to Ft. Leanordwood, Missouri for basic training while Gerda stayed behind with their newborn son. During this time, as Gerda was caring for Ralph, Karl contacted Gerda to inform her that he had been sent papers to head to Germany to be a translator for the United States Army.

Gerda was not receptive to the order. Upon hearing the news, she marched down to the Red Cross, demanding not to send Karl to war. They intended to send him back to Europe for America, and Gerda pleaded that he escaped all the bad things that were happening to refugees like themselves. Additionally, she told them that he could not even speak English, let alone act as a translator. Gerda was once again pregnant, and she relayed how it would be irresponsible and cruel to have her husband go overseas with another child on the way. With enough persistence, Gerda was able to effectively convey her perspective on the matter and Karl was reassigned. Like a good wife, she was defending her love, and trying to ensure that he was there to care and provide for the family instead of revisit the very place they sacrificed so much to escape. The Red Cross assured Gerda that he would not be deployed, but there was no way to circumvent Karl's service in some facet. Uncle Sam wanted him, and he had to oblige. He had to serve two years for a decree set out by the U.S. military.

Karl was sent to Fort Belvoir, Virginia, where he was to finish his training for his servitude, rather than be shipped out overseas. It was tough for Gerda to be without Karl for the first few months of their son's life, but she was able to manage in stride. She continued to work at the World Book, and even got a promotion due to her improved English skills. After completing his stint in Virginia, Karl was officially assigned a new station for the remainder of his term with the U.S. Army at a strategic air command base in Mineral Wells, Texas, just outside Fort Worth. This time, he was allowed to be with his family. Karl returned to Chicago, where he and Gerda packed up the home that they just made their own. Once again, things seemed to be settled, but a change beyond her control altered her plans. Yet this time, she had her family by her side in the safety of America and the circumstances did not have bombs or anything of the sort. This would not be as costly, as the U.S. government facilitated it.

Karl suited for service, 1955.

A FAMILY ON THE MOVE (1955-1957)

The family packed up their car, and began their road trip all the way south to Texas. To Gerda, one good thing about driving with children is that they are always sleeping, except for the times that the parents wanted to get some sleep. About halfway through driving, Karl pulled over to rest at an empty plot of land. He walked out to the middle of the field to get some sleep while Gerda stayed with the baby Ralph in the back seat of the car. When she woke up in the morning, she looked out to the middle of the field where Karl had been sleeping alone. This time, he had some company. About a dozen cows were grazing around him. Karl woke up to the herd of cows mooing and casually hanging about, as he lay dazed. Gerda could not help but laugh, as Karl carefully tiptoed his way around the cows, heading back to the car to finish the ride.

Karl and the boys.

Upon arriving at the military base, the army was extremely accommodating to Gerda and Karl, who were by then pregnant with their second child. After the preliminary salutations were exchanged, a strange anomaly caught one of the senior officers off-guard. He was puzzled about a certain detail pertaining to Karl's military status. Karl, who had already been drafted and trained, was not a United States citizen. The army representative demanded, "Senner! What are you doing here? You are not a citizen!" Karl thought of no other explanation then the obvious truth; "I do not know!" he said. "You brought me here!" This hiccup in protocol was a bit shocking for all parties involved. Karl and Gerda were afraid that Karl could be deported from the United States. The army brass were unsure of how something like this could have gotten through the system, especially given Karl's heritage and the proximity to the end of World War II. Luckily, the problem was solved smoothly and swiftly.

Ralph as a toddler sitting on Gerda and Karl's first car, 1955

Within two weeks, Karl was a United States citizen. Although it was a difficult test that he failed in the process, Karl, despite all his shortcomings in the English language and little experience in America, was able to pass. He was an asset to the United States Army during his short time in the strategic command center. By the time he finished his two-year term, he had been promoted to a sergeant. It is amazing to think that in just over two short years after coming to America, Karl had a wife, child, and a respected position in the U.S. Army, all while not initially carrying citizenship or speaking the language with any sort of clarity. Yet, for all the progress during Karl's service, the most significant experience from this time in Texas was the birth of his second child. Since there was no OBGYN doctor at the base, an ambulance issued by the military took Gerda to Wichita Falls, Texas where she began labor. With much less drama than the birth of Ralph, their second son Michael was born.

Karl in service, 1955.

At the end of his service, Karl and his newly-expanded family headed back to Chicago. There was a statute in the U.S. Army that ensured that anyone who had to leave employment due to the draft would get to retain their job upon their return, so Karl went back to work with the Swede, where he had a job as a mechanic. However, with the new addition to their family, Gerda was pushing Karl to seek work elsewhere for more pay. There was an opportunity with a company based out of

California that was enticing for Karl, and Gerda urged him to pursue it. But Karl's character was that of loyalty and respect. He felt very strongly about leaving the Swede that had faithfully kept him on staff and hired him from the beginning. Even though the money was better in the West, Karl's pride and values were of importance as well, perhaps even more so. Gerda insisted that he at least look into it, and eventually he agreed.

Chapter Twelve

LIFE IN NEW ORLEANS (1957-1972)

Based out of San Francisco, the Enterprise Engine and Machinery Company built and repaired engines for boats and tugboats, and had openings for mechanics. Karl followed through with the interview, and was granted with an onsite consultation in California to determine if he was qualified for the position. Gerda and Karl flew out west for the opportunity that in turn was the first real vacation they had taken together since meeting years earlier. They enjoyed their time on the West Coast, peering out onto the bays and oceans, and reflecting on the fortunate turns their lives had taken. They realized that America really provided much for them, and seemed to only be getting better. There were no obstacles ahead of them, and they hoped Karl's new opportunity was one of many more positive changes to come. As part of Karl's assessment at Enterprise, he was required to build an engine from a collection of all its parts. Karl successfully assembled the engine, but there were some pieces left over. Yet, he apparently impressed them enough because he earned the job. Along with the new salary and position, Karl had to abide by one more stipulation from the company: he was to relocate his family to Louisiana, where the company had a location in the Port of New Orleans. Though they had settled into a satisfying life in Chicago, relocating to New Orleans was a new phase of their lives that they were ready to begin with their family.

OCT 1959

Karl and Gerda in San Francisco, 1959

As the Senners approached the New Orleans skyline in July 1957, from the cold and temperate, Midwestern Chicago, Gerda was only able to think one thing: she had been brought straight to hell. It was the thick of the summer. Gerda and her family had never experienced such excruciating and sweltering heat, only proliferated by the muggy humidity of the deep South. New Orleans was a completely different setting for the German-born family. They had always lived in places with distinct seasons and cold winters. In New Orleans, they found the heat overwhelming. Gerda was in disbelief that these conditions actually existed. This was the next station of their lives, as Karl had just been hired as a mechanic by the San Francisco-based Enterprise

Engine and Machinery Company to work on tugboats in the Port of New Orleans, which was one of the largest shipping outlets in the country, let alone the world. New Orleans, Gerda and Karl soon learned, was an entirely different place than they had been used to in Germany or Chicago, and it was not just because of the weather.

In 1959, Gerda gave birth to her third child, a girl named Heidi. Their house was beginning to fill up in a picturesque way that symbolized the American dream: a hardworking man from Europe with his loving wife, refugees from a tumultuous war, giving birth to three beautiful, healthy children, assimilating into the American culture and beginning to flourish. For the first time in Gerda's life, the tragedy and constant moving stopped. Surely, there would be the normal troughs of any life, but there were no catastrophic events that could derail the life they had. The war was over, and Karl's service was finished. He had a reliable job, and their children were loved in a way that Gerda never was. In Germany, physical and verbal love within a family was scarce. Seldom was it that Gerda was constantly hugged and kissed and told by her parents that they loved her, even though she knew it to be so. However, Gerda made it a point to demonstrate her support and affection for her children, letting them know frequently that she loved them and would do anything for them, more than they would ever know.

The Senners first moved into a home on Calhoun Street in the Uptown district of New Orleans. Their house was nestled in a neighborhood that cascaded with live oak trees sprawling across the skies. Gerda thought the nearby, grand houses of State Street would have been nicer, but it was too expensive for them. With such a big move and a transition into a new job for Karl, it was no time to needlessly splurge even though they were more financially able than in Chicago. Karl worked hard to provide for his family, withholding the traditional German values, where the women were not to work.

Gerda and her boys in New Orleans, LA.

Dr. Donovan Brown, a pillar in the community who later started the Brown-McCarthy Clinic, owned the home. They paid ninety dollars a month for the place where the boys essentially grew up grazing the garbage cans and dumpsters for treasures like magazines and such left behind by college students of Tulane University. The boys would park cars for the games and assimilated into the New Orleans culture as anyone else would. The Browns proved to be more than just landlords to the Senners, but close friends and the reason for Gerda's restitution with faith.

The Browns showed a different side of religion that attracted Gerda to consider the possibility of rejoining the faith, especially for her children's sake. She thought her kids should be given the opportunity to explore faith and be raised in the same context as other children in New Orleans and its many Jesuit schools. The Browns were already good friends, inviting the family over to their grandiose house on St. Charles Street for Christmas. They were members of the Episcopal Church, a denomination that was less abrasive and strict than the Catholic Church. The Browns welcomed the Senners to their church, and they were well-received. For the first time in as long as she could remember, Gerda felt at ease in the church and comfortable with its proceedings. The Senners eventually joined the Episcopal Church and have been members ever since, thanks mostly to the Browns.

Religion was not the only issue that the German natives wrestled with. At this time, segregation was an ongoing controversy in the South. Gerda saw her first black person when she was in New York, and it spooked her then. She now found herself in a former epicenter of the American slave trade and, in turn, surrounded by dissention and racial conflicts. At one point, when they were trying to admit Ralph into a school, in order to attend, Gerda was required to show his birth certificate to prove that there was no deviation of Negro in his blood. This was something that was unfamiliar to them, as Ralph was the son of two Germans, from the Hitler Youth, with blonde hair and blue eyes. But this was how things were during this time. When Michael was a little boy, riding the streetcar, he saw a few black children and told his mother that the kids he saw seemed to look dirty and needed a bath, also commenting how a dirty baby would never be as pretty as his sister Heidi. Just as Gerda was not prejudiced toward Jewish people or those who were persecuted under her time in the Hitler Youth, her children were also not discriminatory of other races. Similarly, they were influenced partly by the social events of their times, unaware of the subtleties of their speech.

For the most part, Gerda and her family could have been mistaken for a number of other model American families, creating living montages of standard American conventions and traditional holidays from Thanksgiving to the Fourth of July. During their time in New Orleans, the only thing that Gerda could complain about was that she was always tired, running after her two boys and managing a household while assimilating into yet another location. Ralph and Michael were typical American boys growing up next to a college. One time, while Gerda was pregnant with her third child, she caught Ralph with an electric razor shaving Mohawks into the neighbor's boy's head. The neighbor's father, a writer for the Times Picayune, reported the story to the news with the caption reading that while Mrs. Senner was taking a cat nap, four boys were in a baby crib, shaving each other's heads. Although nothing devastating, this act was surely memorable and easy to laugh at in retrospect. Another time, Gerda went to check on Ralph to make sure he was sleeping, and found his room empty. The incident was a bit more serious than the Mohawk stunt, and she became extremely worrisome and anxious, frantically searching and screaming for her son.

Just then, a black neighbor, who Gerda had never met before, knocked on her door, asking if her son was missing. Gerda, still frightened, told her that she could not find him. The woman directed Gerda to the gutter where she described a blonde haired blue-eyed boy. Heart-dropping thoughts were circling in Gerda's head until she finally approached her son, playing in the gutter like a sandbox. He had snuck out of his room, down the back stairs, into the street where he was carelessly letting his imagination flow in the gutters of Calhoun Street. Even though New Orleans was a much safer city in the 1950's than it is today, this is a feeling no mother ever wants to experience. She thought back to how her mother tended for her as a child, especially after her time at Potsdam. Minna would do anything to keep her safe, even if she did not show the devotion physically, as was more common in the States.

Gerda experienced one of the most frightening moments of her life soon after the birth of Heidi, one that was in the same lexicon of her darkest days. When Heidi was two years old, Gerda had some company over at night to drink wine with her and Karl. For some reason, perhaps a mother's intuition or a stroke of fate, Gerda went to her bathroom with an uneasy feeling. As she approached the bathroom, she peered into her bedroom, where Heidi was on her bed, seemingly sound asleep. As Gerda picked her up, Heidi did not react. She would not wake or even blink or stammer as her mother held her. Gerda hurriedly went over to her bathroom, where she saw an open bottle of some sugarcoated pills that were prescribed once by a doctor.

Gerda quickly realized the severity of what had happened. Heidi had somehow climbed in to her medicine cabinet, and sucked the coating off many of the pills in the container. Immediately, Gerda rushed Heidi over to Oschner Hospital, where the doctors pumped her stomach and did everything they could to keep Heidi alive. In those minutes, Gerda's heart hurt unlike anything she had ever experienced, even back to the days of war. The thought of one of her children leaving her, and seeing tubes and doctors prying into her body, making any motion necessary to resuscitate the child, was a horror that she had never imagined she would have to endure. Fortunately, Heidi recovered, waking up in the children's ward where the walls were covered with toys and games. From then on, Heidi always asked Gerda if she could go back to the hospital, a place she now associated with fun and games and lots and lots of toys. Calhoun Street certainly had some good memories, as the starting point of their life in New Orleans, but in turn this home was the place of some horrific experiences that stayed with Gerda.

Michael, Heidi and Ralph Senner

LIFE IN NEW ORLEANS (1957-1972)

Although Gerda was undeniably a loving mother, she unwittingly kept some of her own parents' methods into consideration when parenting. Her father's sternness was especially present. Gerda had no problem whooping her children when they deserved it, and was even commended for it. On one occasion, Michael climbed over a fence with some friends to go to a football game in town. The police quickly apprehended them, arresting Michael and taking him downtown to be detained. The police called Gerda to notify them about the crime, and to come get her son. As soon as Gerda came to the station and Michael emerged from the cell, Gerda began, like a true Prussian, to beat her son for being so irresponsible. As Gerda was escorting her son to her car, the police stopped Gerda only to say that they wish that more parents acted as she did. Gerda laughed, saying that Michael would probably prefer to go with the police rather than face his mother, a woman who suffered so much for his life. In the future, Michael even made a deal with some of his friends to keep a stash of money, just in case, to bail him out of jail, so that he would never have to encounter his mother in those circumstances again.

Meanwhile, Karl was doing well at his job with Enterprise, getting a handle on the tugboat business, as well as meeting other people in the ports. He was sustaining a life for his family and was even able to help provide to more than just their children. Gerda, at this point had not seen her parents or sister in nearly a decade. They were living in East Germany under Soviet occupation, which still denoted a communist lifestyle. These conditions would prove to be somewhat beneficial to Gerda's parents. Near their sixty-fifth birthday, they were allowed, and even urged, to leave because they could no longer contribute to society through labor. In a socialist world, the workers help other workers and share the load. At sixty-five, one is no longer useful or capable of helping and is able to leave.

Gerda and Karl decided to bring Minna and Otto over to America, where they could be reunited and live the rest of their days. Karl's mother Helene soon followed suit, and came over to join them. Gerda and Karl had never met each other's parents before, as the two met after leaving their childhood homes behind. With their settled lives in America coming to fruition, Gerda and Karl welcomed their families from Germany to live with them in their home in New Orleans. Gerda soon learned the complications of living with an in-law, let alone one who was mentally unstable.

Karl's mother would utter things to Heidi in German, which Heidi misunderstood as the endearing likes of a grandparent. Once, Heidi asked her mother, "Why is grandma calling me a dummiscamil?" Gerda was upset because this meant "dumb camel" in German. She did not know why Helene would say such a thing unless she was mentally ill. Even just small things, like invasions of privacy, would get to Gerda. Being Karl's son, Helene felt entitled and would persistently assert her influence and presence in the home, saying that the house was hers too. It was difficult for Gerda, living in a full house with her husband, the three children, her parents and now Helene. Not everything could be picture perfect at all times, but she did her best to keep the peace over the thirteen years that they lived together.

Gerda cherished her life in America as well as being able to reciprocate the hospitality and care for her family that was given to her in the traumatic times of her life. However, in light of this positivity, Gerda was continuing to suffer herself, both from her current situation and lurking memories from her past. Gerda, with the stress of her mother-in-law, running a household and getting used to Southern culture, was at a tender point mentally. She consistently would think of her life in East Germany, and all the events that took place that shaped her into the person she was today. She would try to suppress these feelings and emotions and not face them. However, this strategy never proved to be successful. These traumatic events, no matter how she tried to forget them or pretend as if they did not happen, were a part of her. She worked so hard to forget and overcome all of these experiences of bombs and prisons, from physically escaping and running to embracing her many new roles in life. Over time, these suppressed feelings would surface, causing her random bouts of depression and anxiety. Gerda knew she needed to ultimately confront her pain, not ignore it.

She checked herself into the psychiatric ward at Oschner Hospital to seek treatment for the trauma, as well as make sure she was not losing her sanity. The doctor diagnosed Gerda with posttraumatic stress disorder, a condition that is not odd for someone in her position. Her doctor, although sympathetic to her story, saw the strength that Gerda had to summon to overcome all of these experiences, and thrive in a new world and life. It was not that Gerda was going through a tough time in her current station, but that it was all of the truly horrific events of her past that kept resurfacing, having internalized these emotions for so long. Gerda spent her life overcoming and moving past these experiences, so that grieving for them was a process she overlooked. After some time in the hospital, Gerda felt that she had to get away from it. She was ready to keep on going and elected to forego much of the treatment, and the doctor mirrored this sentiment. As she left, he declared, "You were born a Prussian, act like a Prussian!"

Gerda's parents enjoyed being in America. Away from the happenings in East Germany, with his wife, Otto was once again able to enjoy gardening and relax while Minna, too, enjoyed the peace and pace of the South. Gerda even at one point brought Hannelore over, who hated everything about America and returned to Germany soon after. Gerda in a way had become the focal point of her family, establishing a better life in New Orleans where they all gathered under the same roof, as one cohesive unit. Hannelore, though, never found comfort by being inclusive. She said she did not like the people or the culture in America, and talked about how she would hate any life she built in the United States. Hannelore never had the desire to learn English or come to America to begin with, and was satisfied with her life back in Germany.

Michael, Heidi and Ralph Senner, 1968

The house was full and their lives were fully established in New Orleans. Yet, another chance to move would reveal itself. Karl received some unfortunate news that they were shutting down the New Orleans branch of the company. This unexpected turn did not leave Karl without an option for work. Enterprise sent him to another branch in New York to potentially continue working for them there. Karl went to the northeast to check out the details of this new job, and quickly learned that for the size of his family and the cost of moving and then living in New York, the move would be undoable. This left the man with a decision to make. He had to continue working to provide for his entire family, but Enterprise would not be where he took his income.

Karl and another fellow employee, Al Green, decided that they had enough knowledge and experience working with tugboats and its mechanics within the port of New Orleans that they could venture into their own business. Realizing his chance to grab the American dream, Karl set off on his first entrepreneurial endeavor, forming the Green-Senner Company with his partner. With only $300 and a toolbox, the company started as modestly as it could, with little resources besides a small amount of money and their own will and knowledge. The pair began to work out of Green's living room for the finances and business side, while working on tugboats day and night in the ports.

Karl quickly learned heading into this business that the hardest ship is a partnership. He and Green started as colleagues and friends, but conflicting business ideas translated into poor decisions at the expense of their profits and families. Green insisted on not only working on tugboats, but also purchasing some of their own with the earnings. Gerda persistently told Karl that this was an unreasonable move for such a small company. If their business is to work on tugboats and they have to work on their own, they are essentially competing with themselves, she thought. Philosophically, the business model was flawed. But in the partnership, Karl had to appease Green.

Eventually, they bought three boats named The Boaz, The Corinthia, and Dennis. Along with this tenuous situation in purchasing the boats, there were some more core differences between Karl and Green as the company began to predictably lose money. Green had 51% stake in the company while Karl had the remaining 49%, so no matter how much of a partnership was preconceived before the start of the business, ultimately Green had the majority control of all decisions. Eventually, the two had to sell the tugboats. This is where the partnership began to turn sour, and so, too, did the company. The company went under, as did the relationship between Green and Karl. Karl was left with nothing but $300, just like he started with.

During this less than fortuitous venture, Gerda was helping the family, even though true Germans worked hard so that their wives did not have to. Gerda got a job as a bus driver for the schools. Karl did not know about this and when Gerda told him, she made sure to hold the phone away from her ear because she knew how loud Karl would scream. That is how Gerda carried herself as a friend and a wife, regardless of traditional roles. She would help without being asked, and even worked for free for Karl when he needed the help. But, Karl needed more than help when the company went under. He was back at his original position, with $300 and an entire family to care for. He decided to continue in his entrepreneurial spirit, and start his own company working with tugboats. The primary obstacle he had was to gain the business from his previous supplier of tugboat parts out in Germany. This objective was shared with Green, Karl's former parter, who also was pursuing the same supplier for an exclusive business relationship.

Karl and Green were competing for the same distribution, an essential part to each of their prospective businesses, being that the supplier did not need two representatives in New Orleans. On the plane over to Germany to meet with the supplier, Gerda started to smoke again, being so nervous. She was anxious that if this deal did not go through, they would really be in a bad position when they returned to New Orleans. Karl was an excellent salesman and negotiator, but Green needed the business from this supplier just as desperately. By a stroke of fate, luck, persuasion, or some combination, Karl got the exclusive rights to do business with the German company, and was set to start on his own.

Chapter Thirteen

KARL SENNER INCORPORATED
(1972-Present)

Just like his first business had started, Karl began his own venture with three hundred dollars and his entire family to think of. With the business of the German supplier and the tough lessons learned from his time with Green-Senner, Karl started his own company a bit wiser and nonetheless committed. He first decided to name his company Reintjes, which Americans had difficulty pronouncing, later ceding to Karl Senner Incorporated. He rented what Gerda described as a shack on Jefferson Highway. At the time, it was a dump but, it was all they could afford. They had to clean out the space, which amounted to truckloads of trash over hours of effort, eventually transforming the dodgy building into a makeshift warehouse to store parts and play as the base of their operations.

Gerda continued to work for free, supporting her husband in what they all hoped to be a successful job that could provide for everyone in their family back on Calhoun Street. Things were not booming from the start, but slowly and surely began to pick up. Upon starting the company, something amazing happened, a gesture of generosity and faith that not only aided in the inherent business, but also touched the hearts of Gerda and Karl, lasting the rest of their lives. Out of nowhere, one day, three former workers for Karl approached the warehouse, seeking employment. Karl was certainly flattered, but was in no position to give a salary or wage to a worker, let alone three. Conveniently, the men were willing to work for Karl for free.

It could have been that they were desperate for work, or that they knew nothing else but the tugboat industry, but it could also be that the three men believed in Karl. They had faith in his abilities and salesmanship. The men told Karl that they were confident that Karl would pay them when he was able. The worker's acts not only helped with the foundation of the company, but also set the precedent to treat employees as if they were family. All their lives, Gerda and Karl looked out for each other and the people they cared about through the toughest of times. This was an opportunity for them to reciprocate. With a growing business in place, a stable household, and a loving family, Gerda was embracing the American dream that she had envisioned as a little girl. The Senners had established themselves as a lasting presence in New Orleans. With their unique experiences through an exciting journey that brought them to this place at this moment, the notion of community and companionship was always in their minds, and it carried with them in their hearts.

Epilogue

Since the creation of the company, with hard work, determination, and a loyal staff, some that still remain employed today, the Karl Senner Corporation became a thriving family business in New Orleans. Gerda's husband Karl is survived by herself, their three children and their families. When reflecting upon the arc of Gerda's life, it is impossible to think that she did not attain her dreams. She came to America, and also lived up to the ideal of the American dream: starting from nothing and with honesty and hard work, creating a lasting life for her family.

The Senner family began to grow bit-by-bit, not just with their own additions within the family, but also with the close bonds that they shared with workers at the family business. Even Gerda's father had a place in their new life in America, as he enjoyed keeping their garden trim at their church and at the business, like he did in Germany years before. Gerda's maid, Dorothy Learson, was with them for more than forty years and was as much a part of Gerda's life as each experience that shaped her.

Gerda had the pair of black shoes that she had bought from her time on Hermann Farm bronzed, permanently becoming a fixture and symbol of her past. She needed many foot surgeries due to the problems with her shoes as a child. The podiatrist mentioned something to her about wearing the wrong-sized shoes when she was younger. Gerda laughed at his diagnosis, saying how she knew very well all her life that she never had the right shoes.

Gerda went on later in life to reconnect with children from the Hitler Youth and her school. Although many had passed or endured their own unique experiences throughout the war, it was comforting for Gerda to be able to see that others survived as well. Germany and its people were more than the host to many of her traumatic events, but would always be her homeland. At a class reunion, Gerda approached the very same girl who decades before had hosted the birthday party that Gerda was forced to leave. Gerda brought up the incident, telling the woman how at the time, her feelings were deeply hurt and her mother was not a very nice woman. The girl was a snob as a child, and grew into one then, saying how that is just how it was when you do not have the money. To Gerda, it was frustrating to realize that intelligence and ability were not always the most important thing, that sometimes the situation you are in and the circumstances around you can dictate your life more than your own will.

After settling into her life in America, Gerda became more and more informed about the details of the wars by her own research and then watching documentaries. There was so much about the war that she was completely ignorant to as well as some fresh perspectives that helped fill in some holes in her own stories. She felt stupid for being groomed in the Hitler Youth and looking up to a man of Hitler's character. She also felt regret for not being able to intervene with the period's events or act out in a way, which now would seem to be practical and logical. Through her story, it is clear to see that such actions were not as easy as one can assign in hindsight. In fact, being able to speak so candidly and sorrowful about looking back at these times reflects to the purity of her intentions.

Gerda had an apparently fluctuating relationship with faith throughout her life. There were many reasons to question her association with the Catholic Church and even further, with God. When presented the question of the existence of heaven and hell, her response was unique. To Gerda, heaven and hell is not something that is a reward or consequence or even as described in the church, but rather the way you choose to live your life. Heaven and hell is life on Earth. Whether one decides to practice that life in good merit and positivity or in a negative light, it is in these actions that one makes his mark in reality.

The Senners, when financially able, went on to move to a larger home in the suburb of Metairie outside New Orleans on a GI loan where they raised their children in the suburbs of New Orleans. At one time, Karl and Gerda were even appointed the King and Queen of Mid City for Mardi Gras. Standing on stage in costume for the event, Gerda remembers looking at her husband and them thinking toward eachother "How the hell did we ever get here?" Eventually, Gerda built her dream home in Steamboat, Colorado, which was even featured in a home decor magazine for its rustic German design. Gerda made sure to have a template in the entrance of the house saying "We Built This House in the Year of the Lord 1984, Karl and Gerda Senner, Ralph, Michael, and Heidi" further reiterating her sole agenda in life: to live a life with the least amount of suffering, under God, and with her loving family.

Karl Ashby ❤ Bridget Maureen Dunne D'Isernia

Jennifer Marie

Maxwell Clayton

Palmer Addison

Christopher Ralph Senner

Michelle Alexis

Dylan Prescott

Ralph Otto Senner ❤ Christine Roe Senner

Michael Senner ❤ Darci Stugemann Senner

Heidi Senner Means ❤ Clayton Means

Hannalore ⊢— Gerda Suckow ———— ❤ ———— Karl Heinz Senner, Jr.

Anna Paul Wilhelm Hertha ⊢ Otto Suckow ❤ Minna — Hulga Hertha Wilhelm

Karl Sennetski ❤ Helene

References

1. Beevor, Antony, *Berlin: The Downfall.* London; New York: Viking Press, 2002.
2. "List of Concentration Camps and Their Outposts." *German Federal Ministry of Justice.* <http://www.gesetze-im-internet.de/begdv_6/anlage_6.html>.
3. Naimark, Norman M., *The Russians in Germany: A History of the Soviet Zone of Occupation, 1945–1949.* Cambridge, Massachusetts: Harvard University Press, 1995.
4. Nardo, Don, *The Rise of Nazi Germany.* San Diego, California: Greenhaven Press, 1999.
5. Shirer, William L., *The Rise and Fall of the Third Reich: A History of Nazi Germany.* New York, New York: Simon & Schuster, 1990.
6. "Adolf Hitler." *World Book Encyclopedia.* 2011.
7. "Kristallnacht." *World Book Encyclopedia.* 2011.
8. "George S. Patton." *World Book Encyclopedia.* 2011.
9. "Potsdam Conference." *World Book Encyclopedia.* 2011.
10. "Yalta Conference." *World Book Encyclopedia.* 2011.

Thoughts are free, who can guess them?
They flee by like nocturnal shadows.
No man can know them, no hunter can shoot them
with powder and lead: Thoughts are free!

I think what I want, and what delights me,
still always reticent, and as it is suitable.
My wish and desire, no one can deny me
and so it will always be: Thoughts are free!

And if I am thrown into the darkest dungeon,
all this would be futile work,
because my thoughts tear all gates
and walls apart: Thoughts are free!

So I will renounce my sorrows forever,
and never again will torture myself with whimsies.
In one's heart, one can always laugh and joke
and think at the same time: Thoughts are free!

I love wine, and my girl even more,
Only her I like best of all.
I'm not alone with my glass of wine,
my girl is with me: Thoughts are free!

- Die Gedanken Sind Frei

Made in the USA
Lexington, KY
21 November 2012